PROJECT
GIRL

PROJECT GIRL

GIRL

JANET McDONALD

FARRAR

STRAUS AND GIROUX

NEW YORK

Farrar, Straus and Giroux
19 Union Square West, New York 10003

Copyright © 1999 by Janet McDonald
All rights reserved
Distributed in Canada by Douglas & McIntyre Ltd.
Printed in the United States of America
Designed by Abby Kagan
First edition, 1999
Third printing, 1999

Library of Congress Cataloging-in-Publication Data
McDonald, Janet. 1953-
      Project girl / Janet McDonald.—1st ed.
         p.   cm.
      ISBN 0-374-23757-3 (alk. paper)
      1. McDonald, Janet. 1953-   .   2. Afro-American women—New York
(State)—New York—Biography.   3. Gifted girls—New York (State)—
New York—Biography.   4. Brooklyn (New York, N.Y.)—Biography.
5. Public housing—New York (State)—New York.   6. Inner cities—New
York (State)—New York—Social conditions.   I. Title.
F128.9.N4M33   1999
974.7'100496073'0092—dc21
      [B]   98-23281

FOR MY MOTHER, FLORENCE McDONALD,
THE ORIGINAL PROJECT GIRL

PART 1

CHAPTER 1

I live across the Seine from the Eiffel Tower and around the bend from one of the best views in Paris. On my way to work, I pass the gilded bronze statues of the Chaillot Palace that overlooks the Trocadéro fountains. I've been taking the same route daily for more than two years, yet I'm dazzled every time I arrive at this spot. Weekdays, I am in one of my international corporate-lawyer suits, because that is what I do. Weekends, I wear sneakers and my housing-project-style baggy jeans, because that's where I'm from. Through headphones, I might be listening to Missy Elliott or Keith Sweat, or maybe the French crooners Julien Clerc or Véronique Sanson. I belong nowhere in particular anymore and feel comfortable most everywhere.

It wasn't always this way for me. For years, I fought against the undertow that menaces so many of us who grow up poor in America's ghettos. I grappled with all manner of demons, some created by society and others strictly of my own making. My struggle was marred by spectacular failures and salvaged by unlikely comebacks. I was a college-bound project girl as drawn to books as I was tempted by violence.

I grew up in an old-fashioned American family headed by a traditional hardworking father and a tireless mother who stayed home to have children. Seven, to be precise. Luke was the first-born. Still marveling at the miracle of childbirth, my mother soon followed with a second, Ernest. By the time she had delivered Victor and Kevin, numbers six and seven, the only thing miraculous about it all was that she could still walk after such procreative efforts. Smack in the middle of the boys had sprung three girls, of which I was the second, between Ann, the eldest, and Jean, the baby girl. The middle of the middle. A perfect symmetry. And a most unremarkable position if ever there was one in a bustling family.

My parents were children when the Great Depression of the 1930s devastated the world's economy. They missed it. "What Depression? We were always so poor we didn't notice the Depression," my mother said. They migrated to New York in the 1940s, part of an exodus of black people hoping to trade Southern racism and poverty for Northern opportunity. In 1945, on V-J Day, my father, a twenty-two-year-old army veteran fresh from military service, applied for a job as a bus driver in his home town of Decatur, Alabama. The white station manager informed him that Negroes didn't drive buses in Alabama but that he could wash bus windows at the depot. Private Willie McDonald retorted, "I just got out of the army, where I did everything the whites did." He left Alabama that very night in the "Colored" car of a New York-bound train, accompanied by his eighteen-year-old girlfriend, Florence Birdsong. They had only their clothes, a large chocolate bar, and the Brooklyn address of a relative. Within a couple of years, Willie and Florence were married in a ceremony at Manhattan's City Hall.

They were an idealistic Southern couple who believed in the American dream, not so much for themselves—with little formal education, they were realistic about their own prospects—but for their children. We were told to study hard in school in order to get good jobs making good money. "Good" was never defined, but when my father used the term, I knew it meant something grander than sorting mail in the post office, as he did. For my mother, good jobs meant any of the blue-collar jobs held by our neighbors, or, if you were bright and female, a position as a telephone operator, dental assistant, or nurse's aide.

My earliest memories of my father are heroic. There was the story of how, soon after my parents moved into the public housing project named Farragut Houses, a fire broke out in our next-door neighbor's apartment. The mother escaped with her infant daughter, but her twin boys were still somewhere inside. There was no time to wait for firefighters. Daddy dashed into the smoky apartment, holding a handkerchief to his face, and ran out with a screaming baby twin under each arm. As if in confirmation of that feat, the family album contains a photo of him, bulging with muscles, in a cape and tights, an "S" emblazoned across his chest. The bottom of the photo reads: "Coney Island Amusement Park— Brooklyn 1948." For me, Daddy was Superman long before I saw Clark Kent snatch off his glasses to leap tall buildings.

By and by, I learned about life-size cardboard figures with holes for faces, but that information did nothing to alter my belief in Daddy's superhuman powers. I eventually accepted the fact that he was probably not *the* Superman, but he was certainly *a* Superman. He did, after all, seem to know everything. And what he didn't know already, he taught himself. While working full-time as a postal clerk, he mastered Spanish, electronics, cooking, karate, philosophy, shoe repair, sewing, and photography. One of his photos, taken on the Manhattan Bridge above the East River moments before a suicidal man loosened his grip, had been published in a local newspaper.

Although naturally bright, he was haunted by his lack of formal education. By way of compensation, he pushed us to excel in school, and stood poised to bask in our successes as though they were his own. Schooling meant everything to him, and I learned early that it should mean everything to me as well. Fortunately, I had a knack for it. Shining in school was guaranteed to keep me in his good favor, so I shone. My consistently high reading scores attracted the fawning attention of teachers and filled my parents with pride. By fourth grade, I'd already been nicknamed "College Material." The child in the middle of the middle had found a way to stand out, alone and special, in a crowd of siblings. Daddy's expectations were clear. All his children were to go to college and stay off welfare. "A good education is the ticket, and you have to grab it," he said repeatedly.

His naturally loud voice and strong personality at times added a harsh edge to his presence. On family car trips, he'd yell and fume for a navigator but we were all too intimidated by his exacting style to dare attempt reading a map. Mother's calm was a welcome relief from Daddy's intensity. Her ambitions for us were of a completely different order. "All I want is for my children to stay alive and out of jail," she'd say. She joked and clowned so much that often it seemed we were all kids playing together. My father subscribed to the old-school notion that a man's wife shouldn't work. I suppose that, to his way of thinking, a working wife diminished his breadwinner masculinity. So she stayed at home, straightening the girls' hair with a hot comb, barbering the boys' hair with clippers, and cooking, shopping, and visiting neighbors. Such was the life she found "up North," and she liked it.

We lived a Southern life-style in our Northern home. The air hung heavy with oppressive do's and don'ts: do eat all the food on your plate; don't talk back to grown people; do wash your ears and ankles; don't suck your teeth or roll your eyes; do finish homework before watching television; don't hum at the dinner table. Other taboos targeted cigarettes, alcohol, and even coffee, testimony to the simpler world my parents had left in the South. Forbidding the heavier-duty fare of the Northern projects—guns, heroin, and cocaine—hadn't even occurred to them.

Family living was a communal exercise. We watched television together, and went en masse to the public swimming pool, where we learned quickly to shove each other in the pool without being seen by our parents. We also did chores together: one team washed walls, another windows, and a third dishes. My specialty was cleaning the bathroom. True to their Southern roots, Daddy and Mother were excellent cooks, and much of our family time together was spent at the dinner table. No one dared begin eating before each of us had said grace. With hands clasped and eyelids fluttering open just slightly, I would whisper "Jesus wept," keeping a wary eye out for food snatchers. Only then would the feast begin: sumptuous spreads of collard greens, biscuits, green peas, macaroni and cheese, corn on the cob, and fried chicken. Dinner wasn't dinner without a homemade dessert: chocolate layer cake, apple or potato pie, peach cobbler, or some other treat, always made from scratch because packaged mixes were too expensive. Every evening was epicurean rapture.

Punishment was also a group affair, which only added to its sting. Punishable infractions could be anything from zinging eggs out the window, Ernest's way of practicing his throw, to eating all the cherries in the fruit salad, as Ann did, to bed-wetting, my intractable torment. For these lapses, we were whipped with a leather belt. There was nothing worse than glimpsing Ann's subtle smirk as I cried out in pain. Our "spare the rod, spoil the child" Southern parents considered such discipline natural. To us, their Northern children, it was pure barbarism.

Childhood diseases were readily shared. I loved the individual attention being sick brought me, and endured my illnesses with pleasure. While the others had ordinary measles, I had German ones, a distinction that pleased me. Mine *had* to be more dangerous. I might even die. I hoped Mother realized this. The joy of being especially diseased ended when I caught the next one. Luke and Ernest had developed mysterious bald patches on their heads. Soon I had one. The boys got better, but my spot grew. The doctor I visited was stumped and told Mother to wash my hair daily. His advice caused the disease, which we eventually learned was ringworm, to spread, leaving me with nothing but bangs. I was virtually bald at seven years old. Mother blamed herself for listening to "that stupid white doctor," and sometimes I saw her crying as she daubed my scalp with salve. She made cute cotton bonnets in as many bright colors as she could imagine, but they did little against the amused cries and mockery of my schoolmates. Children, though, weren't my only tormentors. Mother stormed over to school one day and angrily threatened to "pull every strand of hair" from the head of the teacher who'd tried to make me remove my bonnet in class. I was thrilled that Mother would brawl for me and hoped to see her do it. My hair grew back within a few months; then I developed anemia. I couldn't walk even a few feet without panting from exhaustion and collapsing on the nearest chair. I was hospitalized for ten days. Nurses drew blood daily from my fingers to monitor my red-blood-cell count. Apparently, I had almost none when I arrived. I once overheard a nurse say mournfully to a colleague, "That little girl almost died." I was delighted. Could anyone be more special, more perfect? The morning I awoke to discover my hospital bed wet, I wished I *had* died. I'd learned from Mother's beatings and Ann's teasing that bed-wetting was the shameful act of a very bad person who deserved punishment. Afraid to lose the affection of my doting nurses, I used the comics section of a Sunday newspaper to cover the wet spot on my bed and sat staring at it for hours, forever. Morning passed, then afternoon, and still I sat. Occasionally, a nurse would ask didn't I want to go to the playroom. "No, thank you, I just want to read," I'd answer with a sweet smile, terrified that I hadn't been good.

In reality, I was quite the "good" child, successfully socialized to be polite, quiet, and to smile at adults. The label "sweet" adorned my head like a halo. I was an angel of "thank you"s and "excuse me"s, a Southern-style little Brooklyn girl. I now regret this early training in stuffing emotions; perhaps having a wider range of expression then would have spared me the destructive outbursts I experienced later.

In contrast, Ann was the family bully who tortured anyone within reach but preferred Luke and me. The pepper-filled hand clamped over my nose so that I couldn't breathe without inhaling black pepper was hers. The voice calling me "yellow" because of my light complexion, or "pissy" when I wet the bed, was hers. It was Ann who squeezed open Luke's softcover diary and ran through the apartment reciting its contents. This was particularly cruel because Luke, skinny and sweet-natured, was a soft-hearted soul who cried to love songs and would do anything for a little brother or sister. Ann wasn't the only one to target Luke. Ernest picked fistfights with him for reasons that probably had more to do with their one-year age difference and a *mano a mano* struggle for dominance than anything else. Ernest regularly won. As resolutely thick-skinned as his older brother was sensitive, Ernest stifled his softer side. It showed though the day he cried after striking out at a baseball game Mother was watching. For my part, I admit that sometimes I was the culprit who ate all the fruit-salad cherries and let Ann take the blame. It was the least I could do to get back at her. Around adults, however, we were good and well-behaved, smothered little creatures secretly lusting to curse, throw things out the window, and play with matches.

The projects were full of kids, and all the adults played parent to all the children. It wasn't unusual for a neighbor to order a rowdy kid home for "acting up." "You ain't my mother" was the usual retort, but we obeyed. Mother's friends visited during the day, when Daddy was at work, and brought their children. The women chatted and drank homemade lemonade while we kids practiced Supremes songs in rehearsal for later performances in front of yawning adults. Christmas was a time to parade new clothes and toys in the hallways, and Halloween an exhausting door-to-door run in homemade costumes and sparkling face paint.

Large families were the norm, and mine felt uncomfortably crowded. I discovered early that books could transport me from our noisy, cramped apartment to new worlds of open spaces and fun adventures. I devoured Nancy Drew mysteries, thrilled to the feats of Pippi Longstocking, and ate goat cheese with Heidi. Maybe the children of the Robertson clan, which numbered around seventeen, did likewise. There were so many Robertsons that the housing authority removed a wall from their apartment so the family could expand into the adjoining one. Mrs. Robertson was a large, silent woman with big bones and broad shoulders who called me "Sugar" in a slow Southern drawl. Neighbors commended her for beating Mr. Robertson every time he came home drunk with no paycheck. Daddy said a woman who beat on a man wasn't a real woman, and called her "low class."

The McDonalds were one of the project's "founding families." When my parents moved into our twelfth-floor apartment in Farragut Houses, the requirements for acceptance were strict. No single parents, no families without a wage earner, and no welfare recipients. The ultimate insult was to shout at someone, "Ya mama on welfare!" There were chained-off expanses of trimmed grass protected by "Keep Off the Grass" signs, neighborhood factories that provided jobs, a flagpole decorated with an enormous American flag, a community center for children, a predominantly Puerto Rican Catholic church, and a predominantly black Protestant one. There was the Boys' Club, the liquor store, several grocery stores, a dentist's office, a pizza shop, a dry-cleaners, and the Brooklyn Navy Yard with its flock of white sailors. It was a time of possibilities—the availability of jobs and good public schools fueled private dreams and aspirations. Everyone wanted to get out of the projects then, too—to an affordable house, a nicer neighborhood, a better life. Later people yearned to get out just to stay alive.

What remains today is the Protestant church, the liquor store, a couple of bodegas, and a bare flagpole. The word "welfare" has lost its sting. The majority of families who live in public housing receive some form of government assistance. Collecting a monthly check, food stamps, and government surplus foodstuffs is no longer viewed as shameful.

Back then, the sense of community was strong because so many activities were done in groups. After school and throughout the summers, boys, and an occasional girl, organized teams to play basketball, punchball, stickball, and something called "Hot Peas and Butter, Come and Get Your Mother." The girls, and an occasional boy, jumped double Dutch and played hopscotch. We knew all the Top Ten Soul Hits by heart and formed singing groups that crooned "My Girl" and "Baby Love" or anything by Smokey Robinson and the Miracles. Ann and two friends donned black sequined dresses and became the Primettes, gaining a certain measure of popularity from the various talent shows they entered. Ann had made it very clear that no, I could not be a Primette, because I was flat-chested, yellow, and pissy. Enviously, I'd sit on the top bunk bed watching as they rehearsed their dips, turns, and harmonies. Ann had so much that I lacked—street smarts, savvy, and ingenuity. I admired the ease with which she confidently talked her way into and out of just about anything, and her ability to find a way to get whatever she wanted, money being the least of obstacles. If she needed new shoes for a dance, she'd talk someone into lending her money. Then she'd buy a pair of foxy high heels on a Friday, dance the weekend away, and return the shoes to the store on Monday. She repaid the debt with the refund. Amazed, I watched her repeat the scam weekly from one store to the next, a brilliant ruse far beyond the capacities of my bookwormish little brain.

My natural ability with words guaranteed success in school. My siblings' talents weren't rewarded in the same way. Luke was gifted artistically but received little encouragement, since, in Daddy's opinion, boys weren't meant to draw and paint. Ernest distinguished himself in sports, a field to which many are drawn but where few succeed; I often played baseball with him and his friends and was proud to be dubbed a "tomboy" because I didn't throw like a girl. Sports skill, however, wasn't what impressed Daddy and he didn't hesitate to condemn Ernest roughly for responding slowly to arithmetic quizzes. Ann's drawing ability and fashion sense would eventually earn her admission into Fashion Industries, the feeder high school for New York's prestigious Fashion Institute of Technology. However, her interest in fashion and singing had little value for a father focused exclusively on academics. And by the time Jean, Victor, and Kevin were making their way through the system years later, the public schools were so threatening that any talents they had took a back seat to the one skill that really counted—survival.

I began school in 1958 and there had my first experience of integration—of sorts. The student body was predominantly black and Puerto Rican and the teaching staff almost exclusively white. But the white teachers had chosen to teach in the projects and cared about their work. They were Irish, Italian, and Jewish, and perhaps had faced exclusion and prejudice themselves. Moreover, the country's liberal political climate encouraged caring about the "underprivileged." We weren't evil or stupid or just plain bad— we simply did not enjoy the privileges others had. The obvious solution was to distribute those privileges more fairly. The "privilege" of adequate basic education, decent housing, and solid jobs would improve American society for all. Teachers embraced this ideal then. With the eighties came the rigid notion of a permanent "underclass." It was no longer a question of what we in the projects didn't *have*—it was what we *were*. Much like India's untouchables, we came to be seen as a class of people destined to be poor, undereducated, and unemployable. It was as though the larger society had decided that such was our collective karma and nothing could be done to change it.

From kindergarten through ninth grade, the years I spent in my neighborhood schools, I had two black teachers. One was Miss Betts, my second-grade teacher, whom I continued to visit over the years, even after I was attending college. The other was Miss Hall, who taught home economics and moonlighted as a bra model. What a racket we made laughing when she proudly showed the class her picture in the lingerie section of a mail-order catalogue—in her underwear!

I was in fourth grade when John F. Kennedy was assassinated. That day a teacher hurried into our classroom, red-faced, leaned toward Miss Higgins, and whispered in her ear. My teacher gasped. I'd overheard what was said. "President Kennedy's been shot." Mother was crying when I got home. Other grownups were crying like babies. "That's a damn shame," Mother said, sighing. "They killed that man because he wanted to do something for black people." Soon, glossy photos of the dead President hung all over—in the grocery stores, dry-cleaners, and our neighbors' apartments. My life was touched by another Kennedy, too. Robert F. Kennedy had come to the projects to campaign with mayoral candidate Abraham Beame. As Kennedy approached, smiling and waving next to

Beame, I grabbed hold of his hand. For a brief instant, his arm tensed. We walked hand in hand all the way down the block, me grinning up at him. I was disappointed that Kennedy never looked back at me. Instead, his eyes nervously scanned the rooftops of the buildings along our path. That haunting image never left me.

A more personal tragedy struck closer to home. Arriving home from school a little later than usual, I was met at the door by Mother, who wrapped her arms around me. "Thank you, Jesus! I thought you was that little girl!" The body of a ten-year-old girl had been found by police. She'd been thrown from the roof of one of the projects' fourteen-story buildings. By evening, all the little girls in the projects had been accounted for except one: Olga Lopez.

I couldn't grasp what had happened. Why would someone want to kill a little girl? Suppose *I* had been the one to go home for lunch, the elevator door opening onto a stranger? What was the meaning of the whispered talk of "sexual assault"? I had no frame of reference for the words. I tried to imagine what had happened to my friend but couldn't—it was unimaginable. Olga's killer wasn't caught right away, which gave us many occasions to run screaming to school. "There he is!" we'd holler. "He's *coming!!!*" The monster we fled in our imaginations turned out to be a quiet sixteen-year-old Boy Scout I used to play with. He gave himself up to the police several days after the crime and ultimately went to a psychiatric hospital. A decade later, I was the only law student in Torts class who personally knew the parties in one of the cases we were studying. Commenting on *Lopez v. New York City Housing Authority*, I turned to a friend from a middle-class New Jersey hamlet. "I grew up with that girl, *and* the killer." She shuddered. "You're kidding! God, Janet, where are you *from?*"

The cycle of seasons rolled on. Autumn brought bright red leaves, fresh loose-leaf paper, and new pencils; winter's snows draped roofs and window ledges in white and heralded snowball wars; spring released its perfumes; and, at long last, summer closed schools and opened neighborhood fire hydrants. On Easter Sundays we wiggled into stiff clothes and absurd hats, and each December applied our best penmanship skills to Christmas wish lists slipped in vain under our parents' bedroom door. I collected certificates of excellence in everything from conduct to science; Luke built delicate replicas of ships from ice-pop sticks; Ernest studied his collection of baseball cards; and Ann drew leggy fashion models and rehearsed with the Primettes.

As for the younger ones, Jean marched with a church youth band, twirling a wooden rifle above her head, and Victor played with his GI Joe doll. On allowance days, they were my best (and only) customers for the Cracker Jack trinkets I steadily accumulated. Ann accused me of greed as I bartered over prices at the ironing board I'd covered with magic rings, figurines, whistles, and temporary tattoos, all gotten as free prizes. Life was good and about to get better.

"Mother, Mr. Mitchell said I'm getting skipped! He gave me this letter!" The parental-consent form I'd brought home authorized the school to place me in the sixth grade a year early because of my high score on the city-wide reading test. "Well, I'll be!" she exclaimed, reading the note. "Like I always say, you got your brains from me. That's my girl!" Then she hesitated. She'd heard it wasn't good for a child to be skipped, that they could develop mental problems, that the older kids would be jealous and cruel. I saw my star fading. "I won't get mental! Anyway, Mr. Mitchell said four other kids are getting skipped, too! So I'll be with my friends! Pleeeze! Mr. Mitchell said I'm really smart! Pul-leeeze!" She sucked her teeth. "Mr. Mitchell this, Mr. Mitchell that. Wait and see what your father says. And don't start that whining!" I got skipped. We were all smart and full of potential—future doctors, executives, and lawyers. But for the moment the five of us were merely new sixth-graders whom the older kids called "mad scientist skanks."

Mr. Mitchell would have been my fifth-grade teacher had I not been skipped. We had an unusual relationship. Whenever he saw me outside of school he gave me a dollar, nothing less than a fortune for a little project girl. Even if he saw me three days in a row. My own father gave me twenty-five cents a week, and that was only if I'd done my weekly chores. Which made Mr. Mitchell's act even more incredible to me. It went like this: I would happen to be walking near the park across the street from school, wearing my holey sneakers. I always wore my sneakers until the cloth tops resembled Swiss cheese. The more holes, the better chance I had of qualifying for a new pair; otherwise, Mother's response was, "Why you need new ones? I don't see hole number one in your old ones!"

Somehow, these little walks always occurred around five o'clock. From the corner of my eye I'd see Mr. Mitchell's white hair and the gray suit he wore daily. One of his shoes had a built-up platform heel and he walked with a limp. "Why, hello, Janet!" "Hi, Mr. Mitchell," I'd say, looking at the ground. "And how are you today?" "Fine, thank you." "Well, you have a nice day, young lady." "Okay." "Here, I want you to have this." "No, thank you." "Really, take it." "Okay. Thank you. Bye." Yes!! Mr. Mitchell's unofficial "allowance" kept me in chocolate cupcakes, potato chips, and Cracker Jacks for weeks!

I'm sure he chuckled each time he saw me just happen to be near school at the end of his workday. Why did he play along with my little game? I always thought it was those worn-out sneakers. But having acted on the same impulse myself, I think it might have been something else. The gesture itself—handing a child money—is perhaps crude. But when I've been back home and looked in the face of some little project kid, knowing what I know about their world and the larger world that awaits them with crossed arms, I've made the same gesture. It's a symbolic but powerful act of generosity and his touched my heart.

Ten years later, Mr. Mitchell's star fifth-graders were caught in the destructive currents of the projects. Jorge was nodding and scratching his way from door to door, selling stolen clothes to support his heroin addiction. Diane's dulled eyes and gray complexion bespoke her drug problems. And Danny, always a little pudgy, had ballooned in size on the methadone he was taking to kick his habit. Vincent had completely dropped from sight, and I was in college, feeling very "mental," indeed. Diane eventually joined Narcotics Anonymous and got clean, but Danny died of an overdose. In a sense, we had been the proverbial best and brightest of the projects. Getting skipped wasn't what dragged us down. The powerful undertow of the new projects did.

The summer after I was skipped, our family took a train trip down South to visit relatives. All I knew about the South was that my parents were from Alabama, and all I knew about Alabama was a song about a banjo. And my mother's stories. She was raised in Decatur, one of seven children herself, all too poor to go to school. She spent her childhood helping her mother clean the homes of white people. My mother never knew her father, who drowned cleaning a well when she was two. The story she had been told was that while my grandfather hollered for help, his white employers stood by and did nothing. Her grandmother was a mean-tempered Cree Indian, and one of her sisters had been murdered by a jealous boyfriend. The young woman's ghost was said to have been seen in my grandmother's apartment, which is where we were going to stay that summer.

I still was young enough to be free of regional prejudice at the time we all arrived at Grandma's place in the low-rise public-housing complex. Adults covered me with kisses, and I had a hoard of rowdy cousins to play with. There were homemade biscuits, crisp bacon, and ice-cold root-beer sodas that my cousins called "pop," and it was all right to say yes to seconds. People called my mother "Ma'am" and me "honey." The red dirt in the playground stained my clean cotton outfits, but I wasn't scolded. I learned to ride a bicycle and played Tarzan with a rope tied to a backyard tree. At first, I was on nervous lookout for my aunt's ghost, but soon forgot her in the swirl of meals, sights, and playmates.

Out shopping with my mother and my aunt, I hopped aboard a city bus and, like any kid, plopped down in the seat with the best view—directly opposite the driver. Smiling and swinging my legs, I watched cars, houses, and trees whir past. The driver smiled. A white woman sitting opposite me smiled. I was pleased grownups were smiling at me, because that meant I was being good. I happened to glance back at Mother. It startled me to see that she and my aunt were frantically waving and pointing upwards. What was I doing wrong? I read "COLORED" printed above their heads. Oops! I jumped up and dashed to the back of the bus. The two women laughed heartily, much to my relief.

I have often wondered why no one expressed anger or resentment, why no outraged explanation was given me, no sense of wrongness conveyed. Perhaps they thought me too young to understand. What is more likely, I think, is that they had been so thoroughly socialized in the South of lynchings, Ku Klux Klan marches, and Jim Crow segregation that whites in front and blacks in the back no longer shocked them. It was just the way things were. And it didn't seem to matter that only a few years earlier the United States Supreme Court had made such racist practices illegal and the Interstate Commerce Commission had ordered the removal of all "White" and "Colored" signs from public buses. Jim Crow was ingrained deep in the Southern psyche.

It was several years before I again set foot in Alabama. The South and I had changed considerably. The "White" and "Colored" signs had been removed from public transportation. Some of my relatives had moved from public housing to their own houses, but always in the same neighborhood—segregation was still the Southern way, only now it was unofficial. The KKK still marched

through Decatur in their white sheets, but people simply laughed
at them. I was a sixteen-year-old high-schooler and had grown into
a Northern chauvinist with little interest in any family that was
not from Brooklyn. The wonderful cousins, aunts, and uncles I'd
met as a little girl seemed dreadfully "country" to me now. First,
there were those silly double names—Bobby Jo, Sallie Bee, Willie
Mae, Patsy Lou. Even the names that stood alone sounded absurd:
Ezekiel. Arneda. Zoralene. Worse, there was the "BP" syndrome:
all my sweet little girl cousins were now barefoot and pregnant.
Patsy Lou was my age and awaiting her third baby, a thought most
distasteful to a bookish, college-bound virgin. I still remember her
bewildered expression that summer as she asked, sweltering next
to me on a porch swing, "Why you always *reading?*" Had I not
been trained always to be polite, I might have replied, "Why you
always *pregnant?*"

But a ten-year-old is readily charmed and at the end of that first
trip down South I couldn't have been more pleased with all things
Southern. Upon my return, I started junior high school and found
it to my liking. Excelling still came easily and school was more
interesting. I took part in a pen-pal program set up with children
in Israel. Until then, my entire universe consisted of the three
square blocks of Farragut Houses. When I received a letter bearing
a postmark from Jerusalem, I studied it with great puzzlement. My
pen pal was a girl my own age named Zippora who wrote about
the weather and her school; I did the same. I was fascinated by
the foreignness of her life.

Music classes were an integral part of the curriculum. At home,
the sounds of Motown filled the children's rooms. Mother hummed
to Sam Cooke and Mahalia Jackson, and Daddy, always the mav-
erick, blasted easy-listening music from windows opened wide on
the projects. He said the projects needed more "culture" and less
"racket." At school, however, the music teacher ruled. "Today
we're going to hear something a little different," she announced

one afternoon. As far as I was concerned, any change from corny folk songs and patriotic jingles was welcome. She placed a record on the record player and passed around its jacket. On the album cover was a drawing of a tribe of massive women straddling wild-eyed horses. The women had uncombed, snake-like hair and wore cone-shaped steel bras. "Class, you are listening to Richard Wagner's *Ride of the Valkyries*. Repeat after me . . ." Taking full advantage of the loud music, the class shrieked, "Rik-*kard* Vog-nuss Ride of the *Valeries!*" "Val-*kir*-ees!" she yelled. I'd never seen or heard anything like it and was captivated. After that experience, I heard the string section in Ben E. King's "Stand by Me" in an entirely new way. Such music would never replace Martha and the Vandellas, or the Four Tops, but I liked it. I recounted music class at dinner that evening and Ann mocked me for liking "whitey" music.

In homeroom, where attendance was taken, I discovered that music wasn't the only difference between my teachers' world and my own. It was the last day of class. Our homeroom teacher was wishing us all good luck when she suddenly burst into tears. "I . . . I feel so bad for . . . your people," she stammered. I was troubled. School was over, summer beckoned, and everyone had been promoted to the next grade. Did she know something I didn't? You bet she did. I have often felt the same sadness when I'm home, hanging out with my teenage nieces, who are all bright and potentially "college material." Yet they are already single mothers, already dependent on public assistance.

Junior high passed in much the same way as elementary school, painlessly. I was placed in a program for gifted students and selected for the math team. The special program offered language study; I chose French because most of the kids had signed up for Spanish, which was widely spoken in our neighborhood. I wanted to be different.

Not everyone in my family was having such a smooth time of

school. Luke passed hours reading in bed but always seemed blue. We thought it was just the ordinary angst of puberty. He was extremely bright and loved to recount tales about the Incas and the Aztecs, yet his grades were unremarkable. Ernest preferred a basketball to a book any day and earned average marks. He made it to the annual city-wide spelling bee, though, but tripped over "phrase," a word Ann worked into mean little jingles for months to come. For her part, routine schoolwork did little to satisfy her creative bent, and the poor report cards she brought home reflected the mismatch. She was only two years older than me, and my easy triumphs galled her, which undermined our relationship further.

The rhythm of school might have felt unchanging and safe, but everything else around me was in frightening transformation. The projects were different from what they had been in the fifties and early sixties. The difference was between low-income and no-income housing, between working families and welfare-dependent single mothers, between adolescent pranks and violent crime.

What began as a neighborhood for the working poor was fast becoming the last stop for the excluded poor. Families with no source of income other than what the State of New York doled out were now qualifying as tenants. "Recipients," snorted my father. He wasn't the only one snorting. Many of the projects' "founding families" were displeased. "I don't like this new breed they're letting in. When I moved in here, you had to have a job. Now all you need is a bottle of wine in your hand." The supply of jobs was dwindling, while the number of unskilled workers was increasing. I saw friends repeatedly go out job-hunting, confident in the value of their high-school diplomas, and return empty-handed. Buddy persevered longer than most. "Janet, listen up, I got this interview down at the docks loading trucks. It looks good. If you still gonna be on this bench when I get back—maybe we can check out the gym." The next time I'd see him, I'd ask what happened. "Oh, the truck thing? Bogus. But the unemployment people gonna hook me up at the gas company." They didn't. He kept looking and updating me on his lack of progress. Eventually, the conversation was always about how much iron he could pump on the bench press. When I'd ask about work, he'd grumble, "Man, ain't shit out there." The decline in jobs for unskilled laborers and domestic workers left a lot of black people with no job prospects, and many found their way to the projects.

The growing "There goes the neighborhood" anxiety created its own version of "white" flight. Instead of white folks fleeing black *arrivistes*, black workers were fleeing the black jobless. "The projects are going downhill. It used to be nice here—before they started letting *them* in," complained those who had come before. As soon as they had saved enough money to put down a deposit on a small house or a co-op apartment in a "nice" area, they moved. Some families returned to the South. The employed were moving out and the jobless moving in. By all appearances, the ship was sinking, and those who could bailed out. I, too, was ready to pack. "Mother, everybody's moving! Can we move?" "Yeah, we can move—as soon as you come up with some 'move' money." I hunkered down for the long haul in this changed environment, now referred to as a "ghetto."

CHAPTER 2

In 1896, the Flatbush Dutch Reform Church donated to the city Erasmus Hall Academy, a private parochial school for boys which subsequently became Erasmus Hall High School. Erasmus Hall, New York State's first public high school, was considered the best in Brooklyn. The school's neo-Gothic quadrangle enclosed a college-style campus. For decades, Erasmians won national scholarships, flowed into colleges, and grew up to be celebrity alumni, such as Earl Graves ('52), the publisher of *Black Enterprise*, the author Bernard Malamud ('32), Barbara McClintock ('19), a Nobel laureate in medicine, and last, and perhaps least, "Happy Days" actor Donny Most ('70), among others. The school also produced track stars, governors, and the first black Miss Universe.

Of all Erasmus's celebrities, though, one graduate's name resounded from generation to generation: Barbra Streisand ('58), the school's own private national treasure. Each new generation of Erasmians claimed her as its own. On vacation in Florence last year, I was standing on a museum line behind an American couple whose distinct accent sang "Brooklyn." The sound so recalled home that I couldn't resist talking to them. They were retired high-school teachers and asked where I'd gone to school. When I said, as I always did, "Erasmus, the same high school as Barbra Streisand," the woman shouted, "I tawt huh! Nice girl." The singer demonstrated her own loyalty to her alma mater in 1994, when she donated $50,000 to the school. It wasn't enough, unfortunately, to keep Erasmus, which had long been in decline, off the list of the city's worst high schools.

But in 1968 there was no doubt about the good fortune that Erasmus represented. The best high school in Brooklyn had accepted me. There was only one problem—it was in Flatbush, a middle-class Jewish neighborhood clear on the other side of town. Erasmus was out of my school district and should have been out of reach. But I was able to attend the famed school—thanks to the Board of Education's Open Schools program, which opened the doors of Brooklyn's top academic high schools to a limited number of promising ghetto students. I didn't *have* to go to a school so terribly far away from home; there were other choices. None of my junior-high-school friends had signed up for Erasmus Hall. I, too, could have attended one of the predominantly black neighborhood schools which offered courses of study in nursing, printing, and mechanics. But not one of these "trade schools," which recruited students presumed to lack college potential, could match the reputation and promise of Erasmus Hall. The presuming was done by the Board of Education, and the students in question were typically black and Puerto Rican. I *had* to attend Erasmus; I was College Material.

My reward for being smart and possibly college-bound was an early-morning hour-long bus ride to a white school where I knew no one. It felt more like punishment. And gave me my first taste of the blessing and curse of academic achievement. The journey to Erasmus carried me across lines of race, class, and culture at a time when I was struggling to patch together some semblance of an adolescent self. Barely recovered from the onslaught of breasts, blemishes, and sanitary napkins, I was suddenly confronted with the first major challenge to my identity as a project girl. The school lent me its very name and, in naming, transformed me. I wouldn't simply attend Erasmus, I would *become* an Erasmian.

Suddenly there I was. It seemed as though everybody cool was sitting cross-legged at the feet of the statue of Desiderius Erasmus, the sixteenth-century Dutch scholar. Pete Goldman's glasses slid down his nose as he pounded out guitar chords, encircled by Nina, Kate, Matt, Saul, the Rosenblum sisters, and a black girl named Judy Casselberry, who was also strumming a guitar. They were singing, clapping in time, and laughing.

> *"Oh . . . well . . . the . . .*
> *white folks hate the black folks,*
> *and the black folks hate the whites,*
> *Oh, but everyone hates the Jews!"*

I was sitting a few feet away with my new friend, Sandy Feldman. I knew whites didn't like people like me, but why would they hate Jews? Anyway, I thought Jews were white, but with Afros, or "Isfros," as they called them.

Sandy was sassy and smart, and dated only black boys, which she said appalled her mother, whom she called a "damn racist bitch." To her face! I shared my confusion with her. "So, how come 'everyone hates the Jews'?" I asked, repeating a bar from the song. She rolled her eyes. "I don't know. Some shit about how we killed Christ." "But I thought Christ was Jewish? Don't they call him the King of the Jews?" "Yep." I was more confused than ever.

If people hated Jews because Jews killed Christ, supposedly, then the haters must love Christ, himself a Jew. So they in fact loved Jews—or at least one. I didn't get it.

Most Erasmians lived in Flatbush, close to school, and didn't hide their suspicions about my origins. "Where, *exactly*, in downtown Brooklyn are you from? The Heights?" they asked, referring to the tree-lined neighborhood of brownstones and sidewalk cafés at the foot of the Brooklyn Bridge. "Uh, no, more like toward the Navy Yard. Do you know where the world headquarters of Jehovah's Witnesses is?" "No," came the answer in a tone that sounded almost like pride. The previous year, my junior-high class had voted me "Most Popular." It was clear that would not be the case at Erasmus.

I was fascinated and overwhelmed. My musical tastes were reeducated to accommodate Jimi, Janis, and Joni. I was so enraptured by Laura Nyro that I wept as only a high-school girl can, listening to her sing at my first concert ever. James Brown, my mother's favorite, had plunged in status, along with Elvis—decidedly not cool. For the first time, schoolwork was difficult, and the other students intimidatingly sharp. I had met the competition and they were fierce. Words tumbled from their fast-moving lips about issues I had never before heard discussed. My fourteen- and fifteen-year-old classmates stridently extolled the virtues of socialism and condemned the evils of capitalism, the Vietnam War, and something we were all supposed to fight against called the "military-industrial complex." I had never even *heard* of a military-industrial complex, let alone how to battle it. At home, my parents rarely talked politics; an occasional barbed reference to "the white man" was as close as they came to political discourse. They admired Martin Luther King, Jr., and had scraped together enough money to send Luke, barely sixteen at the time, to the March on Washington. Malcolm X stirred more mixed emotions. As Southerners who had grown up in the Klan-dominated South of the twenties and thirties, they preferred education and integration to more militant and, to them, dangerous forms of activism. Obviously, the awareness was there; it was the discussion that was absent. Erasmus found me permanently at a loss for the words I had never heard at home.

Eager to learn, I silently hovered at the edges of chatty groups of high-schoolers. People said, "Janet, you never talk! Why don't you ever talk!" I felt ashamed. "I don't have anything to say." In truth, I was intimidated into silence by my sense of utter inadequacy. I preferred listening, especially to Indigo, an art student and self-proclaimed Black Panther who was always decked out in a black leather jacket and matching beret. He had plenty to say and enthralled me with predictions about the imminent armed revolution. My heroine Angela Davis was on the FBI's "Most Wanted" list, and my Afro and wire-rimmed glasses attracted curious glances. I heard so often "You kinda look like that sister they looking for" that I was stunned when years later I attended one of her lectures and got a close-up look at her light-colored eyes and fair complexion, so unlike my own.

The white teachers seemed concerned primarily with the progress of the white students. I was stung by their lack of interest in me and started skipping classes. I faltered academically, failed gym, and was dropped from the math team. Madame Guerrier kicked me out of French class because of three latenesses and was indifferent to my explanation that I lived on the other side of Brooklyn. With typical French fanaticism, she accused me of disrespecting the language and warned me never to take French again. But the most humiliating blow was landed by my drama teacher, who informed me, in an accent rivaled only by Robert De Niro's in *Raging Bull*, that I had no future in acting because of my Southern accent, a sound I associated with dewy-eyed stupidity and dim-witted hospitality. What Southern accent? I wasn't even Southern! I vowed never ever to utter the Southernisms I'd heard at home like "Well, knock me down and fan me with a brick!" or Daddy's incomprehensible favorite, "A hard head makes a soft dinghy," or take leave of someone by saying, "I have to see a man about a horse." I blamed my Southern parents, the obvious culprits. Oh, how they had failed me! No piano lessons, no dance classes, no summer camp in the Poconos. But what do they give me? A Southern accent! It was the final insult in a school career that had gone sour. My only success was in English class, where the teacher liked my written compositions. Small compensation for someone nick-named "College Material."

Heroin had by now made its way into the projects. I learned to recognize the new project look: needle-tracked arms, hands swollen like boxing gloves, gray complexions. The kids who used to sing in the lobbies or play hopscotch on the playground were now teen-agers pushing and using dope. Ann was expelled from Fashion Industries, despite her protestations of innocence, for possessing a "white powder." She insisted she was scratching her nose with a fingernail file. Mother initially let herself be convinced, but I was skeptical. Ernest returned home from his army stint in Germany with a voracious heroin habit; he'd nod out at the table while I was braiding his hair. The ways he and his "homies" found to get money kept them just a few steps ahead of the police—for a while. I was immature enough to find it all terribly exciting, and I secretly admired his "outlaw" behavior. Daddy was angered by all these "shenanigans" and stormed on and on about how everybody was going to end up on welfare or in jail. He was still seething over Luke's recent declaration of his homosexuality and had banished him to Alabama, to "make a man of him." Luke's early adolescent blues suddenly made more sense to me. He'd been struggling with his sexuality in a family of macho men. The news brought tears to Mother's eyes, a sneer to Ernest's lips, and provided Ann with fresh ammunition. I just felt sad that Luke was gone. Now, railed Daddy, the other two were going "straight to hell." Mother said little but kept an eye out for strange behavior, and flushed glassine envelopes down the toilet every chance she got. My Southern parents' early prohibitions against cigarettes, alcohol, and coffee seemed quaint in the new projects.

Everybody had a different explanation of what was happening to the neighborhood. Black Muslims from the Nation of Islam selling *Muhammad Speaks!* preached confidently about government conspiracies, blue-eyed devils, and the drug-dealing Sicilian mafia. Interracial groups of Jehovah's Witnesses went door-to-door selling *Awake!* and cheerfully professing end-of-the-world doom. It certainly felt like doom was upon us. Martin Luther King, Jr., was dead. The Kennedys were dead. Angela Davis was behind bars in the Manhattan Women's House of Detention. A friend nodded out on a bench, sitting on his hands, and awoke with both hands paralyzed. Daddy drilled holes in the front door and added a chain and another lock. Reflecting the times, the Temptations recorded the pro-drug hit "Cloud Nine" and caused an uproar.

Fourteen and penniless, I had few avenues of escape. Until I found golf. Tiger Woods hadn't yet made the game safe for young people of color, so my find did not come without a tinge of shame. Drawn to anything different from project life, I would search the television screen for signs of some other kind of existence. Stretched out on the bed, before remote controls made channel-cruising possible, I consumed whatever a particular channel's programmers fed me. That's how I discovered the Wide World of Sports golf program, with its beautiful green expanses of happy white people in colorful clothing. I was transfixed by a golf championship. Escapist fantasies engulfed me: I was standing in a smooth green field in yellow shoes and red slacks, leaning over a small hole. Ever so gently, I tapped a white ball with the end of my glistening club, and it dropped from sight. The crowd thundered and cameras clicked all around as I leaped victoriously in the air, raced to a nearby pond, and joyously jumped in, the winning club still in hand. Shouting startled me—Ann was in the room. "Janet's in here watching golf! Ha! You a whitey! And get your athlete's stinky feet pissy tail off my bed. *Mother!* Janet's on my bed and she got her own bed!" "*Janet!* Get off your sister's bed! You know you have your own bed!"

Undaunted, I continued to watch golf on television whenever I could. It didn't matter that I understood absolutely nothing, that words like "birdie," "par," and "putt" were meaningless to me. I didn't need comprehension; I needed escape from winos, junkies, and broken elevators. What could be more opposite to all that than professional golf? Gradually, I expanded my television escapes to include performances of classical music, and anything on Masterpiece Theater: the sufferings of rich English schoolboys in short pants and long stockings, tormented by stern headmasters, gossiping servants, and emotionless parents, seemed more manageable than my own.

The contrast between Farragut and Flatbush sharpened as the projects deteriorated and Flatbush remained the same. I was straddling contradictory worlds and not fitting in anywhere. Not in my own family, where I was Whitegirl-in-Residence, not in the new projects, and not at Erasmus, where I was tolerated mostly for the sheer pathos of my "please-be-my-friend" presentation. One day, I was caught stealing albums in a Brooklyn department store. The black store detective couldn't figure out why I had so many copies of the same Judy Collins record and asked me about it. "I was gonna give them to my friends," I said, sighing. What she didn't know was that I already had several stolen copies at home and had returned for more when she snagged me. I could see she felt sympathetic as she lectured me about how you can't buy friends. Instead of calling the police, the usual practice, she called my mother and let me go. Dejected, I took the longest route possible back to the projects. Nothing much was said at home beyond the well-worn speeches about welfare and prison. But good ol' big sister was there to fill any remaining silence. Delighted to see me toppled from my pedestal, she trailed me down the hallway, prancing and whispering, "Klepto, klepto . . ."

Once again, I turned my attention to friendship. Clyde was Erasmus's first long-haired hippie. He was enrolled in my science class but rarely showed up. And when he did, he had an awesome bad attitude. When the teacher asked, "What substance in the mouth helps break down food for digestion?" Clyde answered loudly, "Spit," and walked out. How cool! It had never occurred to me to mock the authority of an adult openly, especially a teacher. His rebelliousness attracted me, as did the fact that he was rejected, as I felt I was, by the more conventional kids. He simply had to be my friend. My strategy was simple: abject groveling. "Uh, hi, Clyde. You don't know me, but I'm in your science class. I noticed you weren't there the other day, so I made a copy of my homework for you." I handed him the neatly copied pages. He stared at me for a long time, then spoke. "Hey. Wow. Cool." The heavens hummed.

Clyde usually sat on the sidewalk in front of the school's gate, playing harmonica, surrounded by an assortment of odd-looking hippies. Fudd was lanky and wore wrinkled clothes. Jewel had a nouveau-gypsy kind of look: ankle-length skirts with dirty hems, and multicolored scarves. Dennis was skinny and his long, matted hair hung in a clump from his small head. I was desperate to be part of their "in" crowd, having decided that Pete Goldman's guitar-twanging clique was "out." Although radical, they were well-behaved little wannabe rebels who obeyed their parents, were very serious about grades and academic rank, and planned for college. None of them had shown any real interest in me, anyway. Even Judy had remained distant, someone I thought should have taken me under her wing in sisterhood. Clearly, she saw little reason to do so, even if we *were* both black. After all, like her friends she was also smart, popular, and lived in Flatbush. And I was pathetic. "Judy, how can I get a really big Afro like yours?" "Judy, could you teach me to play guitar?" "Judy, do you want a Judy Collins album?" Nothing worked. I just didn't have it, whatever "it" was.

Things were different with the hippies; there was no "it" to have. Determined underachievers, they were on the trash end of lower middle class and welcomed anyone who shared their aimlessness. Hippies didn't care about missing classes. I did, but no longer enjoyed school. So I cut, too, which was soon reflected in my falling grades. It wasn't as though I had plans for my future, anyway, so what difference did school make? Besides, Indigo said the revolution was going to make pig institutions like school obsolete, so I was actually getting a jump on things. I bought an army-surplus knapsack decorated with a peace symbol for the books I rarely opened, and donned bell-bottoms, a black vest, and several strings of multicolored beads.

Then it happened. "Hey, wanna get high?" Clyde was looking at me. Hell, no, I thought. I hadn't ever even drank a beer. Drugs were leaving friends slumped on benches and dead in stairwells. I knew a yes would lead to addiction, crime, prison, and early death. "Yes," I said, not wanting to seem uptight. Within minutes, I was sitting on a lumpy sofa in Fudd's basement, holding a joint. Led Zeppelin was wailing about a whole lotta love, and Jewel and Dennis were giggling and blinking slowly. My survival plan was working perfectly, and I felt safe. That is, until Clyde shrieked, "Hey, Janet, what're you doing? You're wasting it, man!" I looked guiltily at my idol. "You're supposed to inhale it, not blow it out! Like this . . ." He drew on the joint and held in his breath. "Oh," I said, my short life flashing before my eyes as I raised the joint to my lips.

I was gradually picking up the jargon appropriate to my bell-bottoms and beads. Phrases like "Power to the People!" and "By Any Means Necessary" and "People Not Profits" fell naturally from my lips. I condemned the military-industrial complex, although I still didn't really understand what it was or how it functioned. At least I knew it was bad. I read *The Autobiography of Malcolm X*, Herman Hesse's *Siddhartha*, Abbie Hoffman's *Do It*, and even tackled the *Bhagavad Gita*. With teenager fervor, I embraced every aspect of the times. I became anti-Establishment, nonconformist, anarchist, revolutionary, socialist, Communist, hippie, yippie, Black Panther, Black Muslim, feminist, separatist, integrationist, Buddhist, Hindu, swirling dervish . . . whatever the era had to offer, I was buying. It was a heady time for a young project girl in search of a broader identity. I protested the war, marched for women's rights, and danced at Central Park Be-Ins, waving my arms in the air. Mother tolerated it all, until I brought home *The Midnight Rambler*.

"You know what we should do, man, we should start a fuckin' newspaper and *educate* people!" Thus spoke Lou Tribe, high-school revolutionary. A bunch of us were loafing on the sidewalk outside school, grooving to Clyde's harmonica. Lou, who looked very much like the young Sal Mineo, was a rebel *with* a cause. His cause was the revolution and he was looking for recruits. "We'll call it *The Midnight Rambler*, like the Stones song." I never saw him in any outfit other than jeans, a denim jacket, and clunky black army boots. He'd written on his army-surplus knapsack: "I Am Waiting for a Rebirth of Wonder." I wrote the same thing on mine. "Everybody will have a task. I'll get money from my folks and contact a place I know in Chinatown where we can get it printed. Jewel, you do layout. Indigo, artwork. Janet, you can write an article." I frowned. About *what*? I knew all the lingo but didn't really *know* anything. "Umm, do you have any ideas, Lou? I mean, like what subjects are we gonna cover, you know, in the first issue? I'm not exactly sure . . ." "Write about the revolution, the fuckin' pigs in the Pentagon, everything! We are going to be the hip alternative to that fascist bullshit paper the school puts out!" Lou buzzed with a zealot's energy. "Sure," I said meekly.

That evening, I sat down with my resources: the Black Panther Party newspaper, the Black Muslim newspaper, *The Village Voice*, and Abbie Hoffman's book *Steal This Book*, which I had done. I strung together enough phrases, expressions, and chants to fill three sheets of loose-leaf notebook paper. The next day I gave my article to Lou. Shortly afterwards, *The Midnight Rambler* was printed and each "staff worker" took home a bundle of papers for distribution later that week. I unlocked the door and eased my bundle into the front closet. What with everyone's shenanigans, Mother had become oppressively wary of all of us. "What are you smuggling into this house?!" she called, that frightful sixth sense of hers kicking in. "Nothing. It's only the school paper." "Then why are you sneaking it in the closet? Bring it here right now!" She took one look at my page-one article and had a fit. "Don't you be bringing no Communist newspaper into this house! You should be studying your schoolwork instead of this mess! If you don't get these papers out of this house early tomorrow morning—and I mean early—they're going straight in that incinerator! You hear me?" I heard her. That night, I lay in bed wondering if Sister Angela had had to deal with fascist-Stalinist-reactionary parents during *her* early revolutionary days.

CHAPTER 3

I spent my summers reading in bed, stoic against the cacophony of music blasting around me. The racket made concentration almost impossible, but I was determined to hold my ground. I had the *right* to read. Mother encouraged me to go outside. "Why don't you go downstairs and get some air, instead of staying cooped up in this room with them books. You know, too much book learning can be bad." "I don't want air," I said, pouting. Mingled in with parental pride in my bookishness were slivers of criticism, defensiveness, and even jealousy. "Book learning" was their favorite insult. Its companion antonym, "common sense," formed the second element of their double-barreled attack. They believed that common sense exists in inverse proportion to academic instruction, a notion that found expression in cutting comments such as "The girl ain't got nothin' upstairs but book learning" and "You got about as much common sense as a speck on a fly!" Deep down, I feared they might be right. Maybe school had so stunted my growth and distorted my development that I'd turned into a sort of project-girl absent-minded professor, a "Mrs. Magoo" of the ghetto. Mother resorted to the book-learning put-down whenever I demonstrated a lack of practical skills. Like the time I roasted a chicken with its paper-wrapped innards still inside. Or when I brought home newly purchased clothes that didn't fit. "How somebody can go to a store and buy a skirt that's two sizes too small beats me! When God was giving out common sense, he ran out just when he got up to you!"

Her own common-sensical side bordered on rabid anti-intellectualism. Books, those things that multiplied from year to year, choking off space like weeds in a garden, were her enemies. And I had accumulated lots of them. "Janet, you better get all these books out my house before I throw them out!" A grim threat for a bookworm. "But, Mother!" "Don't *but* me, cause I don't wanna hear no ifs, ands, or buts. I can't even get into the closets because of all the books piled up in there. If you already read them, I don't see no reason to keep them around cluttering up everything." Her reasoning appalled me. "Mother, you don't throw away books just because you've already read them. Somebody else might want them." She insisted. "I tell you one thing, and I'm not saying it a second time. If you don't do something with all these boxes of books by this Saturday, I guarantee you they'll be in that incinerator come Sunday morning." It was terribly confusing. Daddy insisted I read as many books as possible, and Mother demanded I throw them out. I considered matricide. What kind of person would chuck books? How could such a woman have given birth to me? God, please let me learn I was adopted, I prayed as I lovingly packed more than a hundred hardcover and paperback books into a shopping cart. Lacking only a scarlet "B" on my forehead, I dragged my cart through the projects. People either watched me indifferently or were very curious. "Damn, girl, you read all them

books?" "Hey, bookworm, where you going with them books?"
When I reached the Catholic community center, the nuns looked
at me as though upon an epiphany. Sister Catherine sighed, saying,
"God bless you—such a generous gift." I tried to hide my scowl.
"And do tell your mother Sister Catherine sends her love!" "I
will," I answered coldly, still mulling murder.

My grades were so poor when I finished at Erasmus in 1970 that
I had to attend summer school to qualify for a basic general diploma. It took me an additional semester of evening classes at
Washington Irving High School to upgrade to an academic diploma, a necessity for college. There was also another problem.
Neither I nor my parents knew that I should have applied to colleges *before* the end of high school, so I had missed every admissions deadline. I was a sixteen-year-old high school graduate with
no plans for my life. I had grown up being told I was destined for
college, but with neither direction nor guidance, my future looked
blank. Parental advice—the type of advice that could come only
from a mother who was cleaning houses for food while still a little
girl—left much to be desired. "Why don't you get a job in the
phone company like your little friend Sandy? They pay good
money." "But I'm too young to work!" I protested. Besides, I didn't
know how or where to look for a job, so I dawdled around the
house, immobilized by anxiety, and filled the vacuum with my
usual pastime—reading. I read English literature and psychology
and memorized Sigmund Freud's defense mechanisms and Erik Er-
ikson's seven stages of development. Roller Derby and beauty pageants replaced golf as my most watched television programs, a
bizarre but effective distraction from my predicament.

One night, Ann and I were amusing ourselves poking fun at the
contestants in a Miss Universe pageant when I recognized one of
them. "Look at the black one! I know her—she was at Erasmus!"
I gasped proudly, crawling closer to the television for a better look.
"It's Rochelle!" Two richly gowned contestants were standing side

by side, holding hands. The moment the commentator named the first runner-up, Rochelle's hands flew to her face. "And the winner is . . . Miss Jamaica, Rochelle Pershing!" I couldn't believe it— my former classmate was standing there graciously crying beneath a sparkling crown. My brief flutter of pride was instantly trampled under a rampage of envy. *I* was still in the projects. "I don't remember her being all *that* pretty," I snorted. "Oh, who cares! Beauty pageants degrade women. Who would even *enter* one? But still . . . that shoulda been *me* up there sobbing instead of stuck here in the projects." Ann was supportive, as always. "Don't worry—you'll get your chance at the Miss Pissy pageant," she said, falling backwards, laughing. I felt as if I was a total failure and had to do something quick if things were going to change. But all I could hear was Mother's voice directing me to the telephone company. That is, until I heard that other voice on the soul-music radio station.

The voice—black, male, and smooth—was soothing. "Listen up, brothers and sisters. If you think you have what it takes to go to college but don't have a high-school diploma, come on uptown to Harlem Prep. Pass the test and they'll do the rest." It wasn't quite God informing me I'd been adopted, but it sure came close. The problem was, not only did I already have a high-school diploma, I had *two*: one general and one academic. I hoped they'd take me anyway, and help me find my way to college. I ran to the kitchen, where Mother was washing dishes. "Guess what? I heard on the radio that there's a school in Harlem that'll help you get into college." "Oh, black folk don't know how to run no school," she responded, her Old South upbringing showing. I needed money for transportation. "Can I have subway money?" "No. You don't have no business going all the way up there to Harlem." "Please!" "No." Maybe she was right, but maybe not. This could be my chance to get into college—I wasn't about to let a subway token stop me. Without a word, I left the apartment and headed up the hill, past the Brooklyn–Queens Expressway. As I passed below the elevated tracks, the D train roared overhead. I screamed out loud, something Luke told me he did to vent his feelings. Perhaps everybody wailed under the tracks as they made their way to and from the projects. Years later, a priest was found stabbed to death right there. He, too, might have cried out. But on that day there was only a project girl screaming with hope.

The clerk was busy selling tokens and not a transit cop was in sight. Swiftly, I hopped over the turnstyle, ran down the steps, and jumped on the A train rambling into the High Street station. High Street is an interesting subway stop because it services two very distinct neighborhoods, Brooklyn Heights and Farragut Houses, through two very separate exits. One end of the station opens out directly onto the Heights, home to towering luxury co-op apartment buildings, expensive brownstones, and landmarks like the St. George Hotel and the massive post-office building. Walt Whitman and Truman Capote lived there in different centuries, and various movie scenes were shot along the promenade famous for its stunning views of Manhattan. The Heights even has the world's best pizza, served at Fascati's, a family-owned restaurant on Henry Street that's been around for decades. That is the High Street of the mostly white middle class. Black people from the projects use the opposite end of the station and hike under elevated train tracks and alongside a major expressway before reaching the complex of drab, identical brick buildings that are the projects.

But I had preoccupations more pressing than Brooklyn history as the subway train screeched to a stop at 135th Street. I found the school's address on Eighth Avenue and peered into what looked like, and in fact was, a renovated supermarket. The classrooms were formed by dividers set up in a large open space. The front door was locked, but lights were on inside, so I rang the bell. A gray-haired black man in blue coveralls answered the door, holding a broom. I assumed correctly that he was the custodian and was worried he'd tell me to come back when the teachers were in. "I heard the radio announcement and came to take the reading test." He looked at me for a moment, smiled, and walked off. He came back with a booklet. "You have to take this test. And don't forget to put your name and address on it," he added. The simple reading test posed no challenge, and I completed it quickly. "Somebody'll be getting in touch with you," he said, and saw me to the door. I hopped the turnstyle again and rode back to Brooklyn, breathing hard and making plans. The very next week, I got a phone call from Harlem Prep. The caller's voice carried the sweet sound of salvation—I was in! My parents had muted reactions. Daddy wanted this new school to succeed in getting me into college as it promised, but he seemed reserved. "Well, we'll see what happens, we'll see." For my sake, he hoped blacks could pull off establishing and managing a school. I felt disappointed in them both. It was 1970—Afros, dashikis, and Kwanzaa holiday cards were in abundance, yet they had such doubts. Mother's pointing me to the phone company and discouraging me from going to Harlem Prep had shaken my confidence in her advice—I would not ask for it again. Had I not jumped the turnstyle that day, where would I be now?

Harlem Prep was founded in the late sixties by Ed and Ann Carpenter, educators from Teaneck, New Jersey. I was impressed before I'd even met them, because everyone said they knew the Isley Brothers, singers also from Teaneck. Their titles were headmaster and headmistress, but everyone called them by their first names. The primary aim of the Prep was to give high-school dropouts during the course of a one-year preparatory program the skills necessary to obtain a Graduate Equivalency Diploma and enter college. Funding came from any source available, including private donations, corporate grants, and celebrity fund-raisers. Sammy Davis, Jr., performed at Carnegie Hall to raise money for the school. Grateful alums sent checks when they could. Representatives from

Standard Oil, our largest donor, visited the school periodically, and we were forewarned to be on our best behavior.

The Prep was a hybrid institution, a private school that charged no tuition. Money was always in short supply. The school refused funding from the Board of Education, Ed said, because of the rules and regulations that went along with the money. The faculty was racially mixed and gender-balanced. Some of our teachers held doctorates; others, bachelor degrees. Few had formal teaching cer-tificates, a Board of Education requirement. They were all inspired professionals committed to getting each of the approximately two hundred students accepted at a college. The curriculum differed markedly from that of Erasmus; there was instruction in traditional high-school topics like biology, math, and English, but also classes in Buddhism, African history, poetry, and anthropology. It was as though I had switched from a standard A&P supermarket to shop-ping at d'Agostino's gourmet market.

From the very first day, I loved the supportive, familial atmo-sphere of Harlem Prep. There was a pleasant camaraderie among the students that was new to me. Respect was the value the Car-penters emphasized most, respect for ourselves and for each other. They insisted upon the unity of the student body and encouraged us to view every student's success—or failure—as our own. Ann said each of us was both teacher and student. Ed held weekly community meetings at which he discussed the school's troubled finances, railed against absenteeism, and condemned drug abuse. His discourses were impassioned. "The whole country's eyes are turned toward Harlem Prep. They're all watching us, to see if black folk can pull off this experiment. We're showing the world that our young people, you, are not lost, that you can find your way back into the educational system and excel. We have students from the Prep in the best schools in the country. You're at Harvard, you're at City College, you're at Vassar, you're at Howard. But I'll tell you something—if the man from Standard Oil walks in here and sees half these seats empty, he's going to cut our money. I'm counting on you to be here and be clean. Anyone caught using or selling drugs is out! Remember, you are young, gifted, and black. And we love each and every one of you." His passion and love for us filled me with emotion. I felt his anguish for the Prep's future and his commitment to the students.

Most of the students were black, from backgrounds similar to my own. Yet there was surprising diversity among us, especially for a project girl with little exposure to differently raised black people. Demetrius, a handsome high-school dropout, had grown up riding horses in Connecticut; Kwame, a native of Harlem, had served time in prison. There were Black Muslims, teenagers from New Jersey who owned expensive cars, and students wearing African clothing they had bought in Africa. There were parolees, martial-arts experts, poets, musicians, and painters. Everyone espoused opinions, questioned teachers, and challenged each other's viewpoints, creating an atmosphere that was both exhilarating and intimidating. Early on, I was confronted with my own ignorance by Mtume, a strict vegetarian from a Harlem housing project who meditated twice a day, played African drums, and knew African history in impressive detail. Before the Prep, all I knew about Africa was what I had seen in absurd television movies and on news segments about starvation. As Mtume lectured me about "the white man's willful destruction of the great civilizations of Africa," not exactly dinner conversation in the McDonald home, the gaze of his deep-set, dark eyes grew fierce. I listened silently and signed up for African history class.

There were three white students at the Prep. Their presence inspired a certain ambiguity in me. I knew from my Erasmus experience how isolated one could feel as a minority in an environment such as the Prep's. But I also was aware that, with one step outside, these kids would rejoin the majority and enjoy all the benefits and advantages that white-skin privilege affords. I concluded that whatever momentary discomfort they experienced in an all-black environment was healthy if it sensitized them to how the rest of us felt all the time. Besides, they chose the Prep knowingly, presumably for those very reasons. Once I'd gotten to know them as individuals, however, this internal debate became moot and our relations were not unlike those I had with everyone else.

I enjoyed the company of Philippe, a long-haired Canadian ballet student. He invited me one day to watch one of his dance classes in an Upper East Side studio. I remember a space crowded with young men straining their mountainous thighs in pirouettes and leaps. A petite old Russian woman shouted commands to the sound of ballet slippers sweeping in unison on the wooden floor. I never found out what led Philippe from Montreal to the Prep, but he seemed quite content and at ease. On the other hand, there was Brett, a black wannabe born on the Upper West Side. He dressed in dashikis and African-style *kuffi* hats, and of course played saxophone in a black jazz band. The omnipresent sheen of nervous sweat that collected above his upper lip, coupled with his edgy manner, earned him low popularity ratings. The other white student was a young woman named Rain, who generally kept to herself. Our few conversations, usually about the futility of human communication, hovered in the airless, cerebral spheres where she seemed to spend most of her time, alone.

The school's black hippies befriended me. Ben, a project boy from Brooklyn, was skinny, soft-spoken, and often smelled of alcohol. Daryl and Janine were a couple and knew everything about health foods and vitamins. He had dreadlocks and she wore long skirts. They were black-style hippies, proud of their blackness but not imprisoned by it. Their conception of what it meant to be black was broader and less judgmental than that of our peers. It was all right with them that I loved Joni Mitchell's folk songs as much as I did the Stylistics' soulful melodies. It was all right th Ben was gay and Demetrius rich. No one was "too project" or bourgeois," expressions that conveyed the kind of intolerance Daryl condemned. "We black folks are our own worst enemy. There is no tolerance in our own communities. If you don't talk, dress, or fuck a certain way, you're rejected and marginalized. And we talk about unity!" "I hear that! Each one, teach one," Ben chimed in. Janine had a different perspective. "If you ask me, the first thing that has to happen is you brothers need to respect us sisters. You preach revolution but you don't treat us as equals. Y'all need to put ya sermon where ya dick is. Ain't that right, Janet?" she asked, smiling in my direction. "Uh, yeah. Definitely. Uh, each one, teach one," I stuttered, mortified by the "D" word.

That year I found a kindred spirit in Simone Roche, whose French-sounding name instantly appealed to me. She was an intellectual with strong opinions about racial politics, a combination I admired. She didn't judge or criticize me, and our friendship was comfortable. One time, over widespread objections, she let me bring my little brother Kevin to a party she was giving at her home. While my classmates partied in the living room, Kevin and I finger-painted in a bedroom she'd set up especially for us.

Kevin and I had in fact become inseparable. I couldn't imagine going to Central Park, to Coney Island, or to a movie without him. Sometimes I was downright absurd in my devotion. As we were on our way to a movie one day, Kevin grew tired of walking. He was a long-legged six-year-old, but I picked him up and carried him piggyback-style, as I often did. A black woman walking toward us eyed me as I cheerfully carried my brotherly burden. We came within earshot, and she said, "Girl, get that *big* nigger off your back and make him walk!" A funnier moment could not have been scripted. On another occasion, a Prep student I was dating dropped by to see me in Brooklyn. Kevin sat by my side during the entire visit. When it was time to walk my friend to the elevator, Kevin stood up along with the two of us. "Does your sidekick go *everywhere* with you?" "Yes. He's my little brother." The boy told me

I'd have to choose between the two of them or he wasn't coming back. I chose Kevin.

Our bond was strong, despite a thirteen-year age difference, or perhaps because of it. I was so much older than Kevin that he could not be the troublesome younger kid a slightly older sibling resents having to "mind." He was more a son than a brother to me. In fact, many people, including our own neighbors, thought he *was* my son. Viewed in that light, my relationship with Kevin wasn't as unusual as it looked—I was simply giving him the quality of attention the child in me had missed out on. When we were much younger, Ann and I used to lie on our bunks at night and discuss who was loved more by one or the other parent. The answer was invariably the same—Daddy's favorite was Jean because she was the baby girl, and Mother had a special feeling for Luke, her firstborn. These were the sad, harsh facts of birth order, and the rest of us simply had to accept them. I may have been a shining star for purposes of school, but I was nobody's all-around favorite. And poor Ann—she felt she was no one's favorite for any purpose. I didn't want Kevin to grow up feeling as we had.

My most memorable friend was Joy Carlson, as bold as she was bald. She was very petite and her head was completely shaven. People called us "the odd couple" because we were so different. Joy was loud, aggressive, and could curse with authoritative ease. I was still stuck in my "good girl" persona, the well-behaved child. What shocked delight I took in Joy's unabashed attacks on anyone who annoyed her or dared look too long at her head. "What the fuck you lookin' at, my bald head look better than that knotty clump of shit on your head muthafucka!" She was breathtaking! Imitating her, I practiced enunciation and intonation in the bathroom mirror: "Mo-ther-fu-cker. Motherfucker. Muddafucka." I couldn't muster the same fluidity and conviction Joy had, but I kept practicing. For what, I don't know, since the only place I had courage enough to even say the word was in front of the mirror.

Joy had a dominating personality and could persuade me to do anything. "Janet, you the genius-type. You got the highest SAT score in the whole school. You got it made. I ain't never gonna get in no college if I have to take that fuckin' test. I just can't take tests. Would you take it for me? I'll pay you. Please! We gotta help each other, that's what the Prep is all about." I equivocated. "Yeah . . . I know . . . but I did bad in math. Anyway, don't they check ID?" Her request aroused conflict in me. I didn't want to take the test for her. It just wasn't right. The other students were taking the Scholastic Achievement Test on their own—why couldn't she? But weren't all standardized tests biased against black people and used to oppress us? Why should Joy be kept out of college because of some arbitrary, racist, biased test that didn't really measure human determination? Besides, uptight, preppie white colleges needed bald, rambunctious black women with big attitudes. Still . . . I was black and had managed to do well, so it couldn't be all *that* biased. What would Angela Davis do? I hesitated. Joy insisted. "Fuck the math part. The colleges just care about the English score. I'll give you fifty dollars. You just go in there with all my ID and shit and sit your skinny ass down." I was proud of my SAT English score of 600 out of 800 and flattered by her pleas. Fifty dollars wasn't bad, either. I agreed.

On exam day I showed up at the test site armed with Joy's birth certificate, gas bill, phone bill, and savings bank account identification card. The proctor glanced at the documents and ushered me to a desk. I took the exam as Joy Carlson and later collected my fifty dollars. When the results came out several weeks later, Joy was ecstatic. "We did it!" she cheered, running over to me in school and handing me an envelope. I pulled out the notice and to my horror read "English score—700." Teachers and classmates shook Joy's hand and slapped her on the back. "I didn't know you had it in you!" "Congratulations, Joy, we knew you could do it!" "Right on, little sister. And the top score in the Prep, damn! I should've had you take mine!" It took me weeks to stop grieving for my lost glory.

At the end of my first semester at the Prep, I had straight A's and a renewed spirit—College Material redux. I *hadn't* "gotten dumb," as I'd thought after my high-school debacle. I still had brains and potential. The Carpenters were right: I *was* young, gifted, and black—and perfectly happy where I was.

College-application season arrived all too soon. The Prep had come to feel like family and I wasn't eager to go to any other school. The college counselor was adamant. "Listen, the Prep is a stepping-stone, not a permanent stop. The kids come here for one year, get their act together, and go out there in the world, to college." "I'm not ready. I like it here." He persuaded me to send out applications. "You're already past the deadlines, but I'm sure we can get them waived. We can also get your application fees waived if you don't have the money." I didn't. Grimly, I found a college guidebook and flipped through it. I had no idea what to look for in a college and basically couldn't tell the difference between one school and the next. Some were big, others small, all of them expensive. There were hundreds, thousands, all over the country. Certain names were familiar, most were not. I had no clue as to where to apply, and besides, I didn't want to leave the Prep.

It wasn't merely fear of going "out there," into a world ruled by white people full of negative presumptions about me. I had a deeper anxiety, one I shared with my art teacher. "John, do you think I'm going to turn into a white girl if I go to college?" I was distraught, which is probably the only reason he didn't laugh out loud. "College doesn't change you into someone else. You'll still be who you are, just better educated." His words relieved me, somewhat.

After weeks of analyzing the guidebooks, I selected a college on the absurdest of criteria. "I like the name," I told the counselor.

The name was Briarcliff and it stirred imaginings of Heathcliff's flowing cape and the windswept moors of *Wuthering Heights*. In reality, the college, located in the hills of tiny Briarcliff Manor, New York, was an expensive finishing school for debutantes with horses. The college brochure touted its on-campus stables and stable hands, a perfect choice perhaps for Demetrius and his horses, had enrollment not been limited to five hundred girls. And this was the place I had chosen to spend four years of my life! The counselor frowned slightly and said something about adults making their own decisions. I scheduled an interview at Briarcliff for what I thought was the permanently distant future, but time betrayed me and the dreaded day actually arrived.

I stepped from the Greyhound bus at the Briarcliff Manor depot. Snow blanketed the ground and trees. The few people milling about the station were white. The driver of the lone taxicab parked out front was white. I thought I knew white people, having gone to Erasmus, but these people seemed different. There was an eerie quality of "non-ness" about them: non-cool, non-urban, non-ethnic. Their friendly smiles discomfited me. I approached the cab. "Where to, miss?" "Briarcliff College admissions building," I said, barely audibly. "Ohhh, the college. Real nice place." My head hurt as I stared from the window at the sprawling, split-level houses and big yards bearing down on me. The ride was cruelly short. "Here ya go, admissions! Have a nice day, miss." A black student hurried over to the cab. My hands were trembling. "You must be Janet! Hi, I'm Martine. We're so happy you could make it." Big mistake. I wasn't going to make it *at all*. "Hello," I said stiffly. Blood drummed in my temples. I took a closer look at the girl. There was something about her that was unfamiliar and, thus, disturbing. What kind of name was Martine? And the hairdo—a nappy French roll. She talked funny, too; some kind of accent. Oh, God! They had sent me a black student, but she was no project girl! She wasn't even American—Martine was West Indian! I thought back with hostility to a high-school friend's response to my comments about black solidarity: "I'm not black—I'm Haitian," she'd said. Unsmiling, I scrutinized Martine's clothes for telltale flowers or color clashes. Couldn't they get any real black people? We walked in silence through a long corridor and she left me outside a door marked "Director of Admissions." "When you're done, we'll show you around campus. Have a good one." Who was "we"?

I waited for a long time. No sooner had I leaned my head wearily on the back of the bench than the door to the office swung open, revealing the largest white woman I'd ever seen. She stood six feet tall and had short gray hair, a toothy smile, and pink skin. "Well, hello! You must be Janet!" she shouted, shaking my hand with great force. Why was she yelling? "Give me a couple of minutes and I'll be right out to get you!" Just as abruptly, she was gone. I was acutely aware of my heart's pounding. No way. No way. Just then, the same taxicab pulled into the driveway in front of the building and let out its passengers. I stood and thought for a moment, then went running down the corridor toward it.

The next day at school, the counselor summoned me to his office. "What happened to you up there? You confused the hell out of the admissions director. She said she came out to get you and saw you running down the hall. Based on your record here at the Prep, they were ready to admit you, Janet, if only you had waited. She said that if you want to reschedule . . ." "I'm not ready." He was disappointed, but understanding. Mother didn't seem to mind one way or the other. Daddy, on the other hand, was disappointed and furious. "That was your chance, your ticket out. Nothing but fools in this family. You might as well go on downtown right this minute and sign up for welfare with the rest of the bums who do nothing but eat and sleep, eat and sleep. And I thought you had a brain in that head. Not a lick of sense! You mark my words—a hard head makes a soft dinghy!" By that time, I knew from fruitless expeditions through the dictionary that Daddy's favorite expression had absolutely no meaning—but I marked his words anyway. His frustration was understandable. If he hadn't fathered a half-dozen kids right away, and later a surprise seventh, he could have pursued his dream of becoming a tailor or a chef. But a job with the federal government was a different kind of dream for black people of his generation—one that promised a stable income. That didn't stop him from resenting it, though. What most irritated him were the zip-code exams he was required to take every year. Sometimes he'd have me quiz him the day before; he never missed a code.

My younger siblings were already floundering, snared in the decline of the neighborhood schools. Given the plight of my older siblings, I was his last college hope. The contradiction in his attitudes confused me. He was a man without formal education who valued the life of the mind. But because he was a self-taught intellectual, his attitude toward formal instruction was ambivalent. Ironically, my father's very aspirations ultimately undermined his self-confidence. No matter how many books were read, subjects studied, or skills mastered, he could not change the fact that society labeled him "uneducated." Whence his angry contempt for people he considered "stupid" or "slow," and his mixed messages to a daughter who perhaps he feared might one day come to see *him* as stupid and slow. His conflict did not go unnoticed. I, too, had grown ambivalent about my ticket to success.

Ed and Ann let me stay on at the Prep for an extra year. I avoided thinking about college and resumed my routine along with everyone else. We attended class, did homework assignments, and participated in class discussions. Everything was as it should be, except for the widespread flouting of the Carpenters' anti-drug message, which was heard but not heeded. Erasmians called it pot, but at the Prep it went by the more sophisticated term "herb." Whatever called, it was plentiful. The Black Muslims smoked it in a nearby park while trying to convince a hapless listener, usually me, that Man is the Sun and Woman the Moon and how it meant that sisters need to follow and obey the brothers and what was I doing that weekend? Mtume always smoked at lunchtime—to open himself up to the universe, he said. Demetrius sold it in small packets and began every transaction with "You're going to kill me for the count, but the quality's really good." The packets he sold were indeed rather puny, but I was buying attention, not pot. "Oh, that's okay, Demetrius," I'd breathe, dying to ask him about his world of houses and horses. Afterwards, I routinely gave it away.

But marijuana was not the substance the Carpenters were most worried about. Heroin was. Sometimes Ed or Ann would take a student aside for a private talk. Threats notwithstanding, they didn't really have the heart to throw anyone out of the Prep and would try other alternatives. The guidance counselor and school psychiatrist offered their services to users. Detox programs were contacted. But their efforts were usually met with denials. "I don't mess with that shit. I just smoked a little natural herb." The most visible user at the Prep was Carlton, who commuted from New Jersey in a bright orange Volkswagen bug. I knew the look. It was the same look I saw in Ernest's face after Germany and in Ann's after she left Fashion Industries. At times, Carlton would be so high in class that his head would droop. Someone would chuckle, "Check out Carlton; he is *fucked* up." Another would warn, "Somebody better talk to that brother; he needs help." His girl-friend, Kelly, was also a Prep student and I liked them both. In general, we students saw Carlton as just another one of us who "messed around." His abuse was more extreme than most, but by now heroin use was so commonplace in our communities that only death seemed too extreme a dose.

Ed called an emergency community meeting. We carried chairs from every office and took seats in the main room. He was tearful and Ann looked mournful. I suspected the worst—we'd lost Standard Oil. I had stayed on for a second year and constantly worried that, now that I finally felt ready, the Prep would close before I graduated. "Carlton Jamison was found dead of a drug overdose this morning. His funeral is going to be here in the Prep so that all of you can see what dope does." Ed spit the word "dope" from his mouth like something rotten. That morning, Kelly had phoned the school, hysterical, saying she couldn't wake Carlton. Ed said all of us who turned a blind eye were responsible, especially those who fed, watched, and maybe even participated in his drug abuse. Ironically, Carlton had recently agreed to enter a detox program.

After the announcement, people clustered in small groups, talking about Carlton's death. I remembered with shame my own failure to act. I'm sure others were running similar scenarios through their minds. No one could concentrate in class. "I talked to that brother a *hundred* times about taking that shit. He just wouldn't listen." "I heard they had tried to get him into a program, but I don't know what happened. I think he was on a waiting list." "How could Kelly say she didn't know what the brother was about? She his woman, hanging at his crib all night, and she didn't know he was messin' around? That's *bull*." "I heard they were getting high together." "Damn, that shit's fucked up." The Prep was grieving over a family member's death for which each of us felt responsible.

The day of the funeral, all the cubicles and chairs were cleared away to make room for Carlton's casket and mourners. In a single line, we filed past and took one last look at a young black man, barely into his twenties, already dead. He was at Harlem Prep to get his diploma, go to college, and change his life. Yet there he lay, his gray complexion no different from when he was alive. Big Mike, the jovial biology teacher, shook his bowed head and wiped his eyes. Another heroin user stood a long time at the casket. A teacher had to hold Kelly up as she looked at his body. My throat tightened as I looked into Carlton's waxy face. I saw him nodding at the steering wheel the day he gave me a ride home. I should have said something to him then. But what? I didn't even know what to say to my own brother and sister.

Carlton's death shook me—life wasn't guaranteed, not even for the young, gifted, and black. I decided to stop procrastinating and go to college. Not only was I an A student with *two* high-school diplomas, I had stayed at the Prep for *two* years instead of one. It was time. I showed the counselor a list of colleges that interested me. Lone Mountain College had a poetic name; the University of Hawaii sounded like paradise; and City College was a sure admit. "Why don't you apply to Vassar? They've already taken one of our students and say they'd be willing to take others." I flinched. "Isn't that the school for rich white girls like Jackie Kennedy?" I flashbacked to Briarcliff. "Now, don't start your rich white girl thing again. Vassar is a top school, one of the Seven Sisters, and we need as many of us in schools like that as we can get." I wanted to say, *Then send your mama.* Why did *I* always have to be the one to carry the flag and plant it in foreign soil? He answered my unspoken question. "You're a straight-A student and you did extremely well on the SATs. You're the perfect candidate." Wondering who the "seven sisters" were, I wrote Vassar for an application and fee-waiver form.

It was spring and I was on my way to Vassar College for an interview. After departing from Grand Central Terminal, the Poughkeepsie train makes one more stop, in Harlem, before leaving the city and winding north up the Hudson River. Along the way, it drops off urban professionals who work in Manhattan but raise families in green suburbs. I didn't think about Vassar as I sat gazing out the window at the river and the pretty houses. The quaint Poughkeepsie train station was unpleasantly reminiscent of the Briarcliff Manor bus depot. The taxicab driver pulled through the Gothic Vassar arch, slowed down for an approving nod from the security guard, and left me standing in the middle of acres of verdure and evergreen trees. Ivy crawled up the front of Main

Building, my destination. I exhaled stress. Then inhaled the smell of Christmas and clean air. The inscription above the doorway read: "Vassar College, Founded 1861." Mtume's lectures had sharpened my sense of history. My ancestors were still slaves while Matthew Vassar was worrying about the education of white women. Like Erasmus, this school wasn't intended for me. I learned at the Prep the difference between being wanted and being tolerated. I had nothing in common with Jacqueline Bouvier Kennedy Onassis. What was I doing standing at the front door of her college?

"You must be Janet!" The voice of a WASP. The youthful director of admissions had dark brown hair and a big smile. "Welcome!" His blithe manner reminded me of another director of admissions. I chased her memory from my mind. "Yes," I answered, not knowing what else to say. He led me to his office, chatting about dormitories, language labs, and tennis courts. A student-guided tour had been arranged for me and other prospective students, he said, and some of the black students were very eager to meet me. "Okay," I said, once again waxing articulate. The interview was one of those "So, tell me about yourself" ordeals that leave perspiration stains on your best blouse. There's no telling what a teenager might babble under such stress. Nevertheless, by the end of the interview, I had the impression he liked me, and that made me like him back.

The campus tour was spectacular. I wanted what Vassar had to offer: not the education, but the *life*. Sunlight reflected off the long windowpanes of the central dining hall, the well-groomed golf course stretched beyond the eye's reach, the castle-like library flashed color from its stained-glass windows, and barefoot white kids in cutoff jeans chased Frisbees. Everything I saw was the opposite of the projects. Vassar was a place where you strolled on soft grass, ate as much as your stomach could hold, and lived without fear of muggings, robberies, or assault. And all I had to do was sit in a classroom a few hours a day and write some research papers. What a deal! No wonder white people were so happy. Meeting the black students dispelled the one lingering concern I had about the college. The students I met had not become white at all. They were unlike my own project tribe and my Prep peers—but definitely black. Shenim, a senior, greeted me wearing African dress. Laura, a witty Londoner, cursed as fluently as Joy from the Prep, only with an English accent. The idea of black people in Europe was so incongruous to me that I found myself staring at her. She was cocky and irreverent, or maybe the accent made it seem so. She instantly became the model of how I wanted to turn out if I did go to Vassar: smart, bold, and still black. I had outgrown my prejudice against non-American blacks and identified with Laura because of what distinguished us, albeit in different ways—we were both foreigners. I decided I would attend Vassar if they accepted me.

A few weeks later, Mother made her usual morning stop at the mailbox. She returned carrying a thin letter. "Here, you got mail from that college." She was still holding the six-inch nail she carried for protection against muggers. She'd explained that it offered her the best of both worlds—a weapon that wasn't illegal. I scrutinized the envelope. It was too soon for a decision. Unless, of course, it was negative. I braced myself. Who wanted to be a white girl, anyway? "We are pleased to inform you . . ." I read no further. "Yes!" Mother raised her hands to the heavens. "Well, knock me down and fan me with a brick! My baby's going to college. You know you got your brains from me." "I'm going to be a rich white girl like Jackie Kennedy!" I squealed, happier than I'd been in a long time.

The Prep graduation ceremony was held outdoors because the Carpenters wanted the residents of Harlem to see us graduate. I thought back to my jump over the turnstile two years earlier— who said crime doesn't pay? Daddy stood taller than usual, his broad chest covered with cameras. Mother beamed, repeatedly pointing her Instamatic at the commencement speaker, Ossie Davis. Their pride was ironic. I'd been taught that parents knew best, but in this instance a child, acting against her parents' wishes, had known better. That realization forever changed our relationship. Davis's powerful voice echoed across Harlem, condemning drugs and death, pleading for hope and struggle. I'm sure I was not the only one whose thoughts turned to Carlton, who had come so close to standing with us that day. The Class of '72 sang "To Be Young, Gifted, and Black" one last time, and headed off to college.

Fall had come early, and red and gold leaves colored the campus. A tan station wagon carrying fidgety black people and mismatched suitcases pulled into the entrance to one of the country's most exclusive women's colleges. Aristocratic family names like Rockefeller, Vanderbilt, and Bouvier adorn its graduates like crowns. New-money celebrities like Henry Fonda and George C. Scott send their girls, too, to mingle with the children of doctors, lawyers, and politicians. And alongside these titans was the proudest postal worker in Brooklyn, who had also driven for hours to deposit *his* daughter at Vassar.

My interview visit had not prepared me for that first day. The driveway leading up to Main Building was packed with cars, as were the roads to the dorms, cars piled high with luggage and bikes. The license plates made me nervous. Every rich white girl from Connecticut to California was moving into a Vassar dorm.

"White" and "rich" were synonymous in my way of thinking. Mother reacted similarly. "Ooooh, Janet, you going to school with rich white folk," she whispered in awe. Daddy didn't say much, but he took in the scene as though he were the excited new freshman. "Look at those big, pretty trees," Mother continued, still whispering. I was also intimidated and a touch paranoid. I felt white parents scrutinizing me, to see if I posed any threat to their little treasure. Their kids looked frighteningly white, kids who might have weird names like Kendall or Binky or Pryn. Joy summed up my impressions in a letter she'd written me before dropping out of Southampton Junior College: "They got the *real* white people here." We were in the lair of the big cat—the Wealthy White Anglo-Saxon Protestant. Not so much the real white people as the *really* white people. Or, as Joy put it in her desperate letter, "the ones they got on TV."

Kevin looked at me with big eyes and said, "Wow, you get to go to camp!" Daddy forced me into embarrassing poses in front of wide evergreens and freshly painted pillars. Ernest made cracks about college girls, and Ann reminded me that I was on the verge of an important transformation: "You gonna end up a Straightback Sally." A white girl. We had lunch on campus and moved my belongings into my new room. The time came. Tears threatened to embarrass me—I swallowed hard and blinked. "I'm so proud of you." "Try to give us a short call once a week." "We know you can do it!" The campus reverberated with such classic parentisms as a long line of departing cars inched toward the front gate. Maybe Daddy knew I could do it, but I wasn't at all sure as I hurried up the dorm steps to my room to unpack and ponder.

College was one step along the road to a world of opportunities, connections, and choices for my fellow students. It was for them a means, not the end. Most had at least some notion about their future and Vassar's role in it, whereas my dilemma was Shakespearian. While the others were in college *to be*—stockbrokers like their mothers, lawyers like their aunts, or professors like their fathers—I had been told to go to college in order *not to be*: like my mother or my aunt or my father. The affirmative purpose of college eluded me. Apart from vague talk about a "ticket," no one had ever truly explored with me why I should go to college or what I might study there. From elementary school, college itself had been the future to which I was to aspire. By bringing the only future I had known into the present, Vassar had left me without one.

High school marked the starting line of my class travels. Erasmus belonged to the middle class: its students wore nice clothes and went to summer camp. Vassar was a Monopoly card that read: "Do not stop midway—go directly to Aristocracy." The white Vassar girls wore faded jeans and already had perfect French accents in Beginning French, accents they'd picked up in Europe. The black Vassar girls had grown up in houses, wore expensive clothes, and actually *played* golf. I was as much a sociological oddity to them as I was to the white students. Our differences were so stark that color was all we shared. Blacks constituted an unquantified portion of the ten percent minority enrollment Vassar touted in its catalogue, a figure that included Asians, Hispanics, and others deemed "non-white" by the school. The number of "underprivileged" black students—my natural pool of potential friends—was low, which was attributed to Vassar's preference for black Southerners. I was put off by Vassar's black Southern bourgeoisie; we had little in common other than having been raised in predominantly black environments, which gave us little more than a skin-deep connection. Laura said "niggers from the Northeast" were considered by the administration to be too militant. After all, it was the black *New Yorkers* who had stormed the admissions office in the late sixties with a list of black-centered demands, including one for a black dorm. She introduced me to the residents of the beautiful former faculty residence, redesignated student housing for those black students who preferred to live separately, across the street from the main campus.

Kendrick House gave a new twist to "separate but equal." Much to the resentment of some white students, the black dorm was separate but posh, with spacious, high-ceilinged rooms, far superior to the ordinary fare available on campus. Kendrick's residents were from all over the country. There was Terry, a good-looking, arrogant economics major from California who railed constantly against capitalism. In many respects, he reminded me of Lou and Indigo, my high-school comrades-in-arms. Terry's enemies were "pigs" and "Toms"; his friends, Che and Eldridge. Like Lou, he was rarely seen out of uniform and cut quite the militant figure marching across the Vassar green in his boots, work shirt, jeans, and sunglasses. More approachable was a friendly, soft-spoken black freshman whose mother was Jewish, which, she explained, made *her* Jewish. Paula didn't live in Kendrick House but was there that day, "just checking it out." Perhaps checking out the welcome, as well. It couldn't have been easy to be both black and Jewish in an either/or world, and I admired her poised self-acceptance. I was especially struck by a charming Southerner called Tiny, so named because of his country-boy heft. A native of Mississippi with the drawl to prove it, he challenged my prejudiced beliefs regarding "backwards" Southerners. He was witty, sharp, and one of the stars of Vassar's pre-med program. Dana, a very light-skinned, brash senior, was one of Kendrick's more intolerant residents. She had an aggressive personality and a humorous put-down for just about everyone. Her preferred targets were "those Negroes" who lived in dorms "across the street" and socialized with white students. I suspected she meant me, too; I preferred the easy access to other facilities the on-campus dorms offered and, being a project girl, had a lot less to prove than Vassar's middle-class militants. I was amused to learn much later that

Dana had a white parent; it explained so much about the weighty chip on her shoulder.

No one I met at Kendrick fit into my conveniently labeled boxes or fell within my quick-reference guides. Everywhere, I was confronted with oxymorons: smart Southerners, bourgeois revolutionaries, black Jews, Afrocentric suburbanites, and a very cool black Brit who talked like the Queen of England. Vassar was mind-boggling, which was just what my stereotype-laden brain needed.

Having my own living space was essential. I'd spent my formative years battling Ann and Jean for space in the "girls' room" and relished the thought of having *my* room. At home, I chose the bathroom as my peaceful oasis from clamoring siblings and nonstop noise. I routinely volunteered for bathroom duty and spent hours in that uncluttered, manageable world. Humming, I would sprinkle and scrub the bathtub and sink with cleanser, shine the mirror on the medicine cabinet, and crawl around on my hands and knees washing the tiny, square floor. Off-duty, I'd just sit there and cry. Cry in secret, over too much teasing or too much homework or simply too much commotion. It was a serene spot where I could stand in the bathtub and look out the window. I would watch friends dancing at the chess tables in the back of our building, someone in another apartment ironing clothes, or gaze in the distance at the East River. The bathroom was also the only room in the apartment with a door that locked. Of course, anyone could easily unlock it from the outside and come crashing in, as Ann enjoyed doing, but not if you wedged a mop against the door. That was the closest I had come to having the proverbial "room of one's own"—until Vassar.

Despite my request for a "single," I was assigned to a double room. Fortunately, it was an "alcove room," which is quite different from the traditional two-beds-in-a-narrow-space double. A large, recessed section divided two distinct living areas. The layout

prevented the roommates from seeing each other from their respective spaces unless one stood in the center of the room. Being
the first to arrive, I got to choose the area I preferred. My section
had everything I needed, and much more than I had at home.
There was a dresser drawer, a closet, a bed, a desk, and a chair.
Once I had plugged in Ernest's old record player, put sheets on
the bed, and stuck Kevin's photograph on the mirror, I was set.
The thought of sharing a room with another girl didn't appeal to
me, but I accepted my fate. Maybe she would be a kindred spirit,
a shy, frightened, self-conscious little project girl who didn't have
a typewriter. I would have to wait and see. But suppose she was a
rich, stuck-up white girl. Or a rich, stuck-up black girl. In one of
her letters, Joy told me how a freshman had got rid of her un-
wanted roommate by leaving her panties out to air every night.
Because the potential for embarrassment so greatly outweighed the
slight chance of success, I rejected that option and decided to
enjoy my solitude while I had it.

Which wasn't very long. The rattle of keys shattered my bliss.
Someone else might have dashed over to unlock the door and
welcome the new roommate. Not me. I sought refuge at my desk,
where I picked up a book and pretended to read. The door banged
open against the wall. The sound of bustling footsteps, heavy
breathing, and slamming suitcases left no doubt as to who had
arrived. I stood up from the desk and contracted my cheek muscles
into a fairly decent smile. She was startled: "Oh! You scared me!
I didn't realize anyone was . . ." I struggled against the urge to run.
"Hi, I'm Janet. Need help?" She was black but I could tell instantly
that color was about as kindred as we were going to get. It's not
that I didn't like her. It's just that she appeared so . . . un-project.
"Hi! I'm Brenda. I just got in this morning from California. Do
you know San Diego? It's really pretty! Oh, you're from New
York?! God, I would *love* to visit Manhattan and the Empire State
Building, but New York's so dangerous! Are you from New York

proper?" I had no idea what she meant by "proper." "Brooklyn." "Oh, God, the Brooklyn Bridge is so beautiful—I mean, from the pictures of it I've seen. You're so lucky! *God*, I can't believe I'm here! I gotta call my mom!" Mom? Wasn't that a white-girl term? At home, *we* said "mother."

Brenda and I were desperately different. She was sweet. So was I, but she was sweet with a vengeance. She spoke in a little-girl voice and loaded her side of the room with a confusion of little-girl *things*: metal windup things, stuffed, smiling things, and green furry things that dangled from the ceiling on coiled springs. She had a glossy, smooth perm, clothes galore, a sleek electric type-writer, and an elaborate stereo system that she said I could use whenever I wanted. "God, it was such a hassle getting everything here! When's your stuff arriving?" "All my things are here." "That's *it*?" She shuddered. "Yeah. I don't like clutter," I said de-fensively. "Wow!" Her sweetness was beginning to feel oppressive. I went to my desk and resumed "reading." "Sorry to interrupt, Janet, but come look. Which ones do you like, the ones with the flowers or the ones with the butterflies? I'm sure the rod will be long enough to go across the whole window!" The struggle for power was on. "I don't like curtains." "Come on, they'll be so nice, and brighten up this drab place." Our room didn't look "drab" to me; in fact, I quite liked it the way it was. "I think the ones with the flowers will make it feel really homey! Pleeeze!"

At first, thinking I wasn't serious, she cracked jokes about brib-ing me with food and ready-made term papers. Then she applied herself to begging. "Pretty please with sugar on top!" I didn't budge. Poor Brenda. She just wanted to re-create home, a com-fortable, California house with nice curtains and matching bed-spreads. I *wanted* to be "sweet" but resented Brenda for the life that had led her to Vassar. How dare she have been safe and happy! The flowered curtain *was* nice, but no, there would be no curtains. I agreed, however, to a compromise, and sweet Brenda began college life in a room with a half-curtained window. She told her friends I was "weird" and said the decor of my half of the room was "Early Prison Cell."

Weeks blurred by. I lived off the twenty- or thirty-dollar checks Daddy sent and monies from a combination of grants and loans. I registered for courses indiscriminately: philosophy, biology, religion, psychology, English, tennis. I even enrolled in astronomy, expecting to learn the signs of the Zodiac. What a shock *that* class was. Insecurity led me to select classes in which I had done well at Harlem Prep. The overriding criterion for enrolling in any class, however, was that it not begin before eleven in the morning. I had discovered sleep as a coping strategy and strived to keep my waking hours to a minimum.

The irony of my choice did not escape me—I had deliberately chosen a school far from home, and now I felt lost and fearful. As awful as the projects were in some respects, their world was my home. I had been wrong to split my experience into rigid categories of black and white. My neighborhood was black, but far removed from Brenda's California world of curtains and teddy bears. Blackness was obviously only part of the puzzle. I had left a unique subculture, a universe so distinct that we had our own mores, customs, style of dress, and even our own dialect. We were project people, a tribe apart. And I was apart from my tribe. It was terrifying. So I slept as much as I could. I slept with the determination of a disciplined athlete, until the ache in my body compelled me to get up.

In my classes, I was soon drowning. The déjà vu was disconcerting. As in Erasmus, the work was hard and my peers seemed brighter than I. What about my A average at the Prep? Wasn't I the legendary phoenix, risen from the ashes of high school? What I learned in biology at the Prep just didn't correspond to anything in biology class at Vassar. My first philosophy term paper bombed. The professor looked bewildered. "Your paper was interesting but a research paper should cite footnotes and list sources. It should also be typed." At the Prep, I had written what *I* thought. Why did Vassar want me to quote what *other* people thought? Harlem Prep was nurturing and inspiring, but it had left me unprepared for the rigors of Vassar. I suspect the Carpenters realized the limits of what could be done in a one-year college-prep program and saw their job as getting us through the college doors; once inside, we were on our own.

Mother was my only regular correspondent, and every few weeks I'd get a letter detailing the happenings at home. With the accuracy of a news reporter, she filled me in on all the gruesome details. "You remember the Rivera family on the fourth floor? Well, Rico Rivera was found dead behind the toy factory with two bullets in him. Wasn't he in your class? And your friend Sarah, well, her little brother shot himself in the head. Mrs. Cole from down the street was pushed off the subway platform onto the tracks. The Lord must've been watching over her that day, because the train wasn't coming; she had to get fourteen stitches, though. Did I already tell you that cute boy with the gray eyes, Gilbert Knight, took an OD? For his funeral, the church was packed, and he looked real nice in his casket, just like he was laying up there sound asleep. All the McDonalds is fine. Proud of you." Walking outside, past stately buildings and majestic evergreens, I found a solitary place to sit. After a while, the noise of twigs crackling under approaching bicycle wheels startled me and I quickly blinked the tears from my lashes.

Letters from home usually brought news of this sort; I opened them with a mixture of enthusiasm and dread. Phone calls were often even more upsetting. Luke, now twenty-four years old, had attempted suicide once again over a love affair gone sour. Jean was pregnant and had left school. The family had learned that Ann's boyfriend, the one everyone thought was so nice, had physically abused her. Victor had been chased from the Queens high school where he was bused, by a gang of bat-wielding whites. The litany of misery depressed me, and with depression came guilt. I chastised myself for having abandoned my suffering tribe to learn tennis and philosophy with children of privilege. It was unfair that I alone should be spared. Didn't the others deserve more, too? Why had I been dealt a special hand? I no longer wanted to be special; special meant different, and different meant lonely. The only fair response was to refuse my hand. I would accept neither special nor different. I would be true to my peers, and if they were tumbling downhill, then I, too, would tumble.

CHAPTER 5

The train conductor announced 125th Street as "the first stop in Manhattan—next stop, Grand Central!" It amused me that he didn't say the "H" word—Harlem. The little Harlem station, with its rickety wooden benches and peeling walls, was so different from grandiose Grand Central. I had never gotten off the train at the Harlem stop but was sure I would blend in easily in the black neighborhood. Dressed in my usual jeans and sneakers and carrying thirty dollars Daddy had sent me, I wandered up the broad street, not sure of anything—why I was there, what I would say, how I would be received.

I headed toward a group of tall buildings. Projects. I loitered there for a while, feeling reckless. At last, a young guy approached. "What you need?" His eyes scanned the street. I felt awkward. "Uh, I got twenty bucks." I thought saying "got" and "bucks" would establish me as a homegirl. I might as well have shouted, "Excuse me. I don't wish to be presumptuous, but do you have any heroin for sale, and if so, could you provide me with the quantity/price breakdown?" He smiled. "Where you from, New Jersey?" The ultimate, humiliating insult. "No. I'm from Brooklyn." "Yeah? You seem like you from New Jersey. You sure you not from New Jersey?" His words meant something was terribly wrong with my presentation, that I appeared middle class, maybe even whitegirlish.

A stocky woman with bad skin and glazed eyes approached with an air of no-nonsense urgency. "You straight?" she asked. "What you need?" "Lemme git a dime." He didn't ask *her* if she was from New Jersey. He eased something into her hand as she slipped a bill into his and she split. Straight. Dime. I filed away the new vocabulary words in my memory. The dealer turned his attention back to me; I was ready. "Lemme git two dimes." He slipped two glassine envelopes into my hand, and I fumbled a twenty into his. "I'm on this corner every day, so look for me when you come back. If you don't see me, ask anybody for Eddie." I was so pleased to feel part of this new group that I almost forgot to ask Eddie my second question. "Uh, do you know where I can get . . ." Another vocabulary lapse. "You need works? See that building over there? Go to 1-B. That's Pops' crib. He's cool."

My naïveté was astonishing. I was a Vassar freshman buying heroin in Harlem, without benefit of white-skin privilege, wealth, or family ties. When Robert F. Kennedy, Jr., was arrested in his BMW a few years later doing the same thing, he wasn't prosecuted. I, on the other hand, would have been sent straight up the river, not back to Vassar, but to prison. My existential explanations of tribal yearnings and identity conflicts would have fallen on deaf police ears, as would have my explanation that it was my first time. Neither Carlton's tragic death nor my awareness of the various other risks involved altered my behavior. I was a classic no-common-sense, all-book-learning casualty. Ernest and Ann were doing it, as were a whole lot of my project friends. I wanted to belong, too, make my last stab at being truly *project* before my inevitable transformation into Straightback Sally.

I followed Eddie's directions to the low-rise tenement building and tapped softly at 1-B. A dark eye peered through the peephole. Four locks unlocked, clicking one after another. Absolutely anyone could have been on the other side of the door, but my only concern was the embarrassment I felt. The door opened. Before me stood an old man with black skin and white hair who looked like anyone's sweet old grandpa, except for the enormous revolver protruding from his waistband. Speech failed me. I felt too ashamed to ask something so awful of someone who could be my grandfather. Besides, he might scold and lecture me about the folly of my ways. "Don't be shy with ol' Pops, honey, come on in and make yourself comfortable. No need to be shame with me. You want some works?" I sat on the couch, wanting to throw myself into his grandfatherly embrace and tell him how unhappy I was. Why wasn't he trying to talk me out of it, tell me I was hurting myself, that I should go back to Vassar and stay put? "How many you want, honey? One? Two? They a dollar a piece." I read the marking on the big cardboard box of syringes: "Harlem Hospital." It was a depressing scene, the two of us there, grandfather and granddaughter, with that box.

I wasted no time making a spectacle of myself back at school. To be able to use the works, I had to overcome the fear of needles I'd developed during my annual elementary-school inoculations. But my fear of death stopped me from mainlining, which was how most junkies I knew lived, and died. Instead, I just stuck the needle in my thigh. Most of the time, though, I opted for a less life-threatening route. I scooped the white powder onto the tip of a fingernail file and brought it to my nose, the same gesture that probably had gotten Ann thrown out of Fashion Industries so many years earlier. Bitterness flooded the back of my throat. A warm drowsiness relaxed my body. I cruised over to Kendrick House, where I performed every attention-grabbing act imaginable, short of wearing a T-shirt with "Hey, look at me!" printed on it. I paraded around, wildly exaggerating every sensation. I slumped in a high-backed chair in the middle of the lounge, leaned against the fireplace, knees slowly bending, did a slow-motion doze in the recreation room. I wanted everyone to know that I was not like them, and would not become like them.

It wasn't long before I was known for having "a problem." As much as I pursued my own isolation, I loved the attention and solicitude I was getting. "How long you been on that stuff?" I was asked. "Oh, a long time. I'm from the projects, you know," I lied. Laura lectured me in that darling accent about one-way paths and dead-end streets. Terry said I was needed for the revolution and shouldn't destroy myself. But my battle was elsewhere. I told myself that my act affirmed my project-girl identity and proclaimed my solidarity with the downhill plungers I left in Brooklyn. In reality, my actions bespoke the distorted reasoning of a guilt-ridden survivor.

Most people shook their heads in disapproval but said nothing. Maybe they felt as awkward as I had at the Prep, watching Carlton nod and drool. Harriet, the black belle from Tennessee, had plenty to say, however. Her clothes and manner commanded deference. I could see she was someone used to the best. She wanted to "try it" but needed to know it was "good quality." I assured her it was top-notch. Eddie had said so. She wasn't entirely convinced. "It's not cut with any shit? I mean, I won't get sick, or jump out the window, will I?" Sniffing it was perfectly safe, I asserted. "Okay. Can I do some with you? But don't tell." She didn't want me in her room, so we went to the Early Prison Cell. Brenda was out, as was often the case. I suspected it was because of me, but she said she just had lots to do. Harriet asked when the rest of my things were going to be delivered. "Never," I said, chuckling. We got high. A few moments passed. Harriet had a puzzled look on her face. "I don't know, I feel kind of weird. I had some once before, but it felt different. What kind of coke is this?" "Coke? That was heroin . . . I thought you knew." The belle bristled. "Damn, girl! Nobody takes *that!*" After that incident, whenever we crossed paths we would look at each other and burst into laughter. The reaction "across the street" was altogether different. A couple of my white friends, hell-bent on waging their own brand of rebellion at Mom's alma mater, were desperate to experiment. Taking "smack," as *they* called it, with a black girl from the ghetto was the kind of thing that made breathtaking journal entries. And all within the safety of the ivy-wrapped walls of Vassar. Wasn't that what college was about, the enriching experience of meeting people from different backgrounds?

A wealthy friend from the Upper East Side begged me to share some with her. Adrian was all curls, dimpled cheeks, and aristocratic airs. Recalling Harriet, I was more reluctant this second time around. "Suppose you overdose and die? It'll be my fault." I remembered the suspicious look I thought I had seen in the eyes of white parents my first day. "Oh, for Chrissakes, dahling. I've taken more of everything else than you could even *dream* about. What's a little smack going to do to me?" Her characteristic way of punctuating sentences with the word "dahling" annoyed everyone but me; it reminded me of Masterpiece Theatre. I was given a similar line by pencil-thin Pearl, the banker's daughter from Palm Springs. She insisted she'd taken it before, but gave a suspiciously vague description of what the high felt like. She even wanted to go with me to Harlem, having "heard so much about it." It was as though the entire trust-fund set of Vassar College wanted to be teenage junkies.

Finally, I agreed to share. But absolutely no one would be allowed to make the trip with me. "You'll attract too much attention, like walking spotlights." Always the pushover, I returned to

Harlem, accompanied by Pearl and a buddy she'd brought along, a German intern. They were to wait in the 125th Street station until I got back. All three of us must have looked like "walking spotlights," huddling and whispering in the waiting room. "Just sit here and don't move! And don't try to make friends. I should be back in about half an hour." Pearl told me to please be careful, and the German said, "You're so brave." Foolish was a more accurate description. My Vassar admirers didn't know how easily I was outmaneuvered by *real* project folks. It wasn't unusual for a dealer to take my payment, then direct me to wait in an empty lobby or at a nearby car, tree, or trash bin—anywhere other than near him. Inevitably, he'd disappear. I came to know from the sound of someone's promise to "be right back" that he wouldn't. When I accepted that something, or perhaps everything, about me spelled "easy target," I began bringing extra money to replace what would invariably be ripped off. There was nothing I could do but sidle over to the next unsavory-looking stranger, hoping for the best.

I didn't see Eddie anywhere and asked for him as he had told me to do. The response was blunt and indifferent. "Eddie locked up. What you need?" I got what I needed and went to see Pops again. I knocked at his door. A neighbor opened hers. "He ain't there no more, honey. Pops got killed. A robbery." I stood there dumbfounded. She closed her door. Pops had been shot dead by someone who wanted free syringes and fast money. How could someone kill a gentle old man? I couldn't help thinking that maybe he, like me, was also out of his league.

I was away longer than expected. When I walked into the train station, there was not a Vassar girl in sight. "Did you see two white girls around here?" I asked an old woman in the restroom. She looked at me suspiciously. No, she hadn't. I caught the next train to Poughkeepsie and arrived late in the evening. I found Pearl and the German in the campus café, drinking beer. We squealed and hugged. They'd left after waiting for an hour, because the ticket clerk kept staring at them, as though they were "prostitutes or something." We went to Pearl's room and shared what I'd bought.

Education had taken a back seat to my identity drama. The only class that held my attention was English. The professor, Judy Kroll, was typical of Vassar's impressive faculty. Not yet thirty, she had published a book of poetry and already had her doctorate. We were on a first-name basis, an informality I had learned to appreciate at the Prep. Like mine, her identity was a mix of diverse influences. Originally from Queens, she was married to an Indian academic whom she'd met at Dartmouth. A frequent visitor to India, Judy often wore saris, shawls, and sandals to class, which seemed very exotic. Celebrity worship best described my feelings, and I felt the delicious rush of a teenage groupie whenever she drove by in her black Mustang convertible, blowing the horn and waving to me. My fellow classmates were envious. "You're friends with *her?!* But she's so aloof to everybody. What's she like?" "Nice," I'd respond with false nonchalance. I was thrilled when Judy asked me to help proofread the manuscript of a book she was writing on Sylvia Plath, and then felt petrified that I might miss a typo. I had never met a published author and basked in reflected glory. She welcomed student visits during office hours and seemed to take a genuine interest in our talks about life in Brooklyn and my lack of direction.

In English class, she presented the works of Virginia Woolf, Anne Sexton, and Sylvia Plath with subtle intensity, and the discussion explored questions of identity from the perspective of these writers. I spent long hours studying the reading material and laboring over my term papers. Something in me resonated to their struggles, despite our obvious differences. On my own, I read Maya Angelou, Zora Neale Hurston, and Toni Morrison. A larger identity was taking shape, expanding beyond the project-girl persona I embraced.

Like movement along a fault line, this inner shifting threatened my stability. I sought calm all too often on Harlem's street corners. Despite, or perhaps because of, my glaring lack of sophistication, most people I met were nice to me. Nonetheless, it was impossible to establish any lasting relationships because folks like Eddie and Pops vanished from one week to the next. My school relations had failed, not surprisingly, given my acting out, to blossom into genuine friendships. And somehow I'd made myself believe that college posed a threat to me but the destructive behavior and caricatures on which I was basing my identity did not. Despair creeped into my soul.

Brenda was out of the room. I turned on the record player and put on a recording of Beethoven's "Moonlight Sonata." Then I sat down on my bed, holding a bottle of sleeping pills prescribed for what I'd told the local doctor in town was insomnia. I had decided to die. Thinking in the absolutes typical of depression, I found "everything" sad, overwhelming, and hopeless. The somber piano chords filled my head with grandiose notions of tragic and noble young death. I swallowed two pills and looked at myself in the mirror. No, the glasses had to go; I would look cuter without them. I placed my glasses on the dresser, beneath Kevin's photo. It hit me how pathetic I was, a coed whose closest relationship was with her kid brother. I took a few more pills. Again, I looked at my reflection. Maybe I looked better *with* the glasses, more intellectual. I put them on, and washed down another handful of pills. Now I was scared, but there was no turning back: I had already taken so many that if I didn't finish myself off, I was sure to end up a bedridden vegetable. The bottle empty, I lay down on the bed and waited for drowsiness and death to envelop me.

A half hour passed. Nothing was happening. I put on another record for ambiance, Samuel Barber's "Adagio for Strings." I continued to wait to be whisked away to the happy heaven of young poets and rock stars. After an hour without even the slightest yawn, I realized I had been duped. Placebos! I thought angrily. The doctor was probably used to Vassar students coming in with fabricated complaints. More dollars down the drain. I was also relieved, as much as I didn't want to admit it. No one was happier to have lived to tell the tale than I was, recounting my failed suicide attempt the following day to the mental-health counselor. For my own safety, I was confined to the infirmary. The same day, I unscrewed the window screens of the room and climbed out, took the bus to the station, and hopped the train to 125th Street. Back at school that evening, I skulked around campus, dodging campus security cars, high and content with myself. I called Judy from a phone booth in Main Building. She said, "Everyone's looking for you." After a long conversation, she was finally able to persuade me to return to the infirmary.

I opened my eyes the next afternoon and looked directly into Daddy's heavy face. Mother and Kevin were there, too. Vassar had put me on a medical leave of absence. Then I *really* wanted to die. Glum and disoriented, I got dressed. Mother and Daddy had already packed up my belongings, so I didn't even get a last look at my Early Prison Cell room. Four months after my momentous arrival at college, I was on my way home. The brake lights of the tan wagon shone red as Daddy slowed down to let pass a bus marked "West Point Weekend," full of Vassar girls. As they got off and disappeared across campus, we pulled out and headed toward the expressway. The bike I had "found" outside a dorm and repainted black lay strapped to the top of the car. Silence resounded, except for Daddy's dire third-person predictions. "She's gonna end up just like that dope addict girl on the second floor, what's her name, the one in jail?" From the back window I watched Main Gate recede from view. I was banished from the castle, a project girl again, in fact as well as fantasy.

What felt like a one-car funeral procession turned onto a Brooklyn street. Upstairs, I went to my "room of one's own" and sat for a long time on the side of the bathtub. It had been traumatic to leave home to be resocialized and reeducated in an alien world. But it was worse to be back as a failed college girl. I realized it was far better to be *from* the projects than *in* the projects. Like Icarus, I had flown high and suffered a spectacular fall. College had given me a glimpse of a wider, whiter, wealthier world than my own. I wanted to assume its benefits, but not its identity. Did I have to *be* it, to share in it? That was the conflict that had wrestled me down and threatened to pin me there, in the projects.

CHAPTER 6

I spent my semester off writing letters to friends on both sides of Main Street, and to Judy, who had become mentor, friend, and faithful correspondent. I still have all her letters. "You're keeping the post office in business all by yourself," said Mother, impressed by the dozens of letters I mailed out each week. I had grown up with a love for words and writing. I'd spend hours scribbling stories about rebellious girls. My first book, entitled *Build House on Island*, was an ambitious work held together by staples. Inside I listed Things to Eat, What to Wear, and Toys and Books to Have. I was most marked as a writer by my first childhood diary, which I carefully hid from Ann, in light of her mischief with Luke's. In the opening entry, I breathlessly recounted how a seventh-grade classmate I had a crush on sang to me on the school bus. "Please, God, make it all true!" I gushed on paper. Mother's voice crashed down on me, a wall of humiliation. "You shouldn't leave your diary laying around, especially if you're gonna be writing about your little boyfriends." She'd read it! I immediately went to the incinerator and dropped the black book down the chute. Now the memory of that act stopped me from keeping a diary, but not from writing letters. And I did so feverishly. My correspondents were the only people I talked to openly.

As a family, we shied away from discussing personal issues, so my situation was left to speak for itself. I assured my parents I would work harder at Vassar when I went back, and stay out of trouble. End of discussion. But much was expressed in my father's crestfallen glances and my mother's heaping plates of food. "You want more greens? You eat like a bird. That's probably why you went up there and showed your tail. You have to eat more."

Home felt empty. Luke had discovered hip-huggers and platform shoes and lived in Greenwich Village. Ernest was locked up in an upstate prison. He and a friend had been arrested in connection with a robbery in the Heights. Since Ernest had chosen to go to trial rather than plea-bargain and was not a cop's son like his buddy, he took the hardest hit and was sentenced to twenty years under a new Draconian anti-crime law. At the time he was twenty-three, with no criminal record. Ann was selling hats and clothes she designed and sewed herself, to get money for drugs. Of the young set, Victor had found deliverance from the projects with Uncle Sam and was stationed somewhere in the South, and Jean was living on a lower floor in our building. Undaunted by the struggle of raising two daughters alone, she battled on, getting both her diploma and a job as a secretary. She made sure her daughters had the latest in clothes, toys, and computers and was fiercely determined to send them both to college.

Kevin was thrilled to have me home. He expressed it daily, popping in my room with a candy bar hidden behind his back. "Janet, guess what I got for you!" I was profoundly disappointed in myself and continued to fantasize about suicide; one day I brought up the topic with Kevin. "If someone were really sad all the time and things looked like they would never get better, do you think that person should kill herself so as not to be sad anymore?" He thought for a while, bringing his entire eight and a half years of life experience to bear on the question. "No, because they wouldn't be able to eat or play anymore." The simple logic of his philosophy was seductive. I stopped thinking about death.

I avoided hanging out in the neighborhood because I hated hearing, "Hey, college girl! Good to see you! How long you gonna be home?" Not only had I let down the family, I told myself, I had failed my community by robbing them of a role model. In truth, I had never really been a role model for anyone. People saw me as a sort of brainy freak, someone unlike themselves, an "other." Among those who knew what had happened, the reaction was along the lines of, "So what, you fucked up. Since when is *that* out of the ordinary in the projects?" A leave of absence from college was laughably negligible compared to prison terms and dope deaths.

Slowly, I began to realize that the person I'd really let down was myself. I wrote. I read Dr. Seuss books to Kevin. Judy called when she was in the city to meet with the editor of her Plath book. We would lunch in Central Park, visit the zoo, and talk about her writing and my plans for the future. The only plan I had was to get back in college, but my fragile confidence had been shattered in the fall from grace. Judy had "no doubt whatsoever" that I belonged at Vassar and could succeed if I applied myself to the work. As for my fear of changing, she reassured me I would simply become more of myself in college, not anyone else.

Volumes of letters were mailed and delivered daily. An envelope came with my dreaded first-semester grades. Three incompletes and a B in Judy's English class. I was thrilled. If I could earn a B in a Vassar course despite my turmoil, what might I accomplish in a more serene state? It was mid-May and I still felt fragile. I'd been seeing a psychiatrist recommended and financed by the college. Week after week, Dr. Silver sat ensconced in a deep leather chair, tilting her head one way, then another, mum. And every month she sent Vassar a bill for services rendered. I was impressed. The practice of psychiatry seemed to be a scam much slicker than any devised in the projects—big money for little effort, and no results required. She was no help at all. I needed desperately to grab hold to something before giving school another try, and all she could do was play mime. Where was divine intervention when you needed it? As it turned out, it was in Wysox, Pennsylvania.

I decided to run away to the Big Sur and live on a commune. Unhindered by minor details like my lack of money and California contacts, I checked the "Rider Wanted" ads in *The Village Voice*. Steve the bearded driver and King the blue-eyed Alaskan husky were en route to San Francisco in a rainbow-painted van and needed a rider to share expenses. I had scrounged together only forty-five dollars but trusted that the Big Sur peace and love crowd would take care of me. Steve and I arranged everything by phone and agreed to meet in a week at the Washington Square arch. I climbed into the passenger seat and settled in for my first cross-country trip. I inquired about the photo swinging from the rearview mirror, of a pudgy boy with slicked-back hair. "That's Guru Maharaj Ji," said Steve. The seventies were chock full of gurus, but I hadn't heard of this one.

Against the backdrop of New Jersey turnpike scenery whizzing by, I savored the exhilaration of my reckless lunge from thought to action. I had done something, taken action. Free-falling, probably, but at least in motion. Steve turned to me: "Jan, right? I promised some friends in Pennsylvania I'd stop by. They're really blissful." His words instantly vaporized my euphoria. He hadn't mentioned anything earlier about a stop. I didn't like the idea at all. "Okay, that sounds cool," I said, thinking: I don't want to die!

Dusk was descending on the tiny farming village of Wysox as Steve pulled the van onto the lawn of a simple two-story house. Inside were a pair of married refugees from Wisconsin and their son, another married couple, a single mother and her son, and a frightened kitten cowering in the bathroom. Initially, I went unnoticed in the flurry of hugs, kisses, beards, ponytails, and foreign words. Then one of the women said, "Hi!" and Steve suddenly remembered me. "Oh! Jan, right? Meet the greatest people in the world." He recited a list of names, but the only one I remembered was the kitten's. Christie. "Jan's riding with me to California." His friends said, "Blissful."

We sat down to a dinner of soybean burgers and fresh vegetables from their garden. I noticed a framed picture of the same round-faced boy perched on the living-room mantel in the middle of a circle of candles. Anguish spread through me. I had seen farm people in movies and knew what they were capable of doing with their wood chippers. This group didn't look like homicidal maniacs, but you never knew. Ted, a former sociology professor, worked as a landscaper. His wife, Marlene, stayed at home with their young son. Ron worked with Ted, and together with his pregnant wife, Gail, owned the house. Doreen and her baby son received public assistance. They were all around thirty years old, and very curious about me. Marlene eyed me kindly and asked in a sweet voice, "So, Jan, what are you going to do in California? You have friends there?" I said no, and looked at the kitten. Gail said, "Oh, I guess you're gonna see family." The image of Kevin offering me a candy bar shot through my mind. Maybe it was fatigue, or fear or my first soybean burger . . . I burst out crying. "I'm running away from home and I have no idea what I'm going to do!" Marlene put her arms around me, radiantly compassionate. "Don't cry! You can stay here, Jan, with us. It's so clear that you were sent! Blissful! That's how Guru Maharaj Ji works! Thank you, Steve, for bringing Jan to us." Then they all began chanting the foreign words, which I subsequently learned were "Bole Shri Satgurudev Maharaj Ki Jai!" and meant "All Praise due to the Perfect Master!" I looked around at the joyous white faces smiling at me. They weren't going to kill me, after all! I smiled back. "Okay." I wrote home and said I was fine and spending the summer with "some friends" on a farm. My hosts were eager to meet my family and extended an invitation to them. My letter didn't mention the teenage guru.

They described themselves as *premies*, or devotees, of Guru Maharaj Ji, the then fourteen-year-old Perfect Master. They meditated twice a day and regularly visited area ashrams to sing the guru's praises. I focused on enjoying my surprise summer in the country, weeding the garden, planting vegetables, and making soybean burgers and granola with Gail and Marlene. I even had my first driving lessons. When I knocked over a wooden mailbox, overreacted, and bumped into a slow-moving oncoming car, the *premies* didn't mind. Just Maharaj Ji up to his little pranks, they said.

I took long walks on empty roads, splashed around with my hosts in cold creeks, and lolled on the grass under the broad blue sky. Ted told me an old neighbor asked about "that charming little Negro girl" staying at the house. She wanted to know if I was from the Fresh Air Fund. We got a good laugh out of it. I didn't laugh, however, when a little white girl walking in town answered my smile with a stuck-out tongue and the word "Nigger!"

Daddy accepted the invitation, and my heart leapt when I saw our station wagon pulling onto the property. Mother, Ann, Jean, and Kevin climbed out, sniffing the clean air and looking around as if for something to look at. This time it was my turn for wild hugs and kisses. The *premies* met the McDonalds and we ate lunch together. Afterwards, Daddy and Ron strolled between rows of corn, talking about the vegetable garden. Kevin played with the other children, and the rest of us just relaxed. No one said anything about my running away from home. I think Mother and Daddy were just happy that I was all right. As for the rest, they'd wait and see. I said I had every intention of returning to Vassar, which pleased them. Everyone enjoyed the weekend and my family departed with happy expressions and bags of vegetables.

In July, the *premies* drove to New York to attend a talk by one of Guru Maharaj Ji's mahatmas. These saffron-robed "saints" were said to transmit wisdom to aspirants through a touch of a finger on the person's forehead. At that moment, you were supposed to see within a bright inner light of divine Knowledge. The *premies* wanted me to be initiated by "receiving Knowledge." I wasn't sure. In my opinion, a white *premie* was one thing, but a black one from the projects, well, that was quite another. In the end, uncertainty yielded to anxiety. Despite feeling much happier and settled than I had in a year, I was still worried about returning to college. I decided, what the hell, I would ask for the Light, just for backup. In a plush *premie* apartment on Central Park West, we listened for hours to the mahatma's discourse. He spoke of maya, or illusion, the treachery of rational thought, and Maharaj Ji's wisdom. When the time came, I raised my hand along with a number of others who felt "ready" to behold the Light. The shades were drawn and we sat in meditation. I was abruptly startled by a finger touching my forehead. I wasn't sure I saw anything, but it didn't matter. The important thing was that I was officially "saved." A baby-faced guru was watching over and protecting me. I meditated side by side with the other *premies*, worked "blissful" into my vocabulary, and handed out Guru Maharaj Ji leaflets in nearby cities. In Philadelphia, we nearly scuffled with some Hare Krishnas who accused the Perfect Master of being a materialistic, false prophet who wore gold jewelry, drove a Rolls, and needed to get on a diet.

In September, I returned to college, with much to prove and a giant framed poster of Guru Maharaj Ji's face for my wall. I was assigned to Kendrick House. Some students received me with skeptical courtesy, others with outright disdain. Politically oriented black students sought to convince me that Maharaj Ji was "irrelevant." Pearl, Adrian, and the rest of my old friends were delighted to see me back, although they didn't quite get the "guru thing." Laura had graduated and occasionally sent encouraging letters. Judy Kroll was on a year-long sabbatical in India but continued to write me regularly. I was on my own.

It being my second try, I was actually a *faux*-freshman and hoped the college's real freshmen wouldn't hear about my disastrous first year. Registration was a breeze the second time around. My priorities had changed. In defiance of my high-school French teacher's command, I enrolled again in French class, this time despite its early-morning scheduling. The reality of social diversity supplanted my clichéd world of "rich white girls" and "bougie blacks." Of course, Vassar wouldn't be Vassar without its share of debs, heirs, and trust-fund brats of all races, but a surprising number of them were down to earth. Moreover, there were other kinds of students, if you looked. Along with Pearl and Adrian, my friends included Fabienne, a *very* rich black girl from Harlem who drove a red Mercedes convertible and was as unpretentious as any kid from the projects. I also got on well with Suzanne, a Jewish art major from Long Island who was on financial aid; Urvashi, an outspoken feminist of East Indian origin with a wicked sense of humor; and Gray, a Puerto Rican from New Orleans who sang like Aretha in the school's gospel choir. I realized I was no more an outsider than an Indian feminist or a Puerto Rican Southerner or a Harlem teenager who kept horses at her family's upstate ranch.

Armed with the divine Light and a second-hand typewriter, I was ready. I attended classes, pored over thick English novels and thin books on religion, corresponded with Judy in India, and practiced my tennis serve, which never improved. I hadn't chosen a major, but that could wait. I just wanted to succeed as a student. Daddy's monthly checks arrived, as did Mother's weekly letters. The bleak stories from home sometimes slowed me down to a sullen churn, but I maintained my forward momentum. Kevin spent weekends with me sometimes and met my friends, bowled in the school's bowling alley, ate himself into a stupor at Central Dining, and cheerily sang along to my Guru Maharaj Ji records. He thoroughly enjoyed Camp Vassar.

I got to know the one other *premie* on campus, a debutante from Baltimore, and together we would go to the ashram to "testify" and sing "The Lord of the Universe." But my faith was brutally dashed to bits at the Houston Astrodome Divine Light Festival. A chartered planeload of us flocked to Texas to see Guru Maharaj Ji himself, his blessed mother, and his four holy brothers. The buzz in Houston was that the Perfect Master was going to transform the Astrodome into a gigantic flower-bedecked spaceship and whisk us off to nirvana. I was ambivalent. After everything I had been through, I wanted at least to finish college before making the celestial trip.

Swathed in white, Guru Maharaj Ji gazed down upon thousands of *premies* from a satin-draped throne. Amidst cries of "Jai Satchitanand!" and "Blissful!" he spoke about rainbows, nectar, and light in a slightly irritating, high-pitched voice. *Premies* in locked lotus position swooned to and fro with eyes shut. The less flexible, like me, tried to hold the locked L position—legs straight out and back erect—but ended up shifting incessantly on the hard floor. Following the discourse, I waited for two hours to pay my respects to the Guru's mother. In spite of my best efforts, I couldn't stifle my growing embarrassment as I stood in line, and felt thankful that nobody from the projects saw me kiss her miniature white-socked foot.

The Astrodome failed to lift off, which left a lot of *premies* disheartened and a few suicidal. The longtime devotees argued that the Divine Teenager himself had never explicitly said the Dome could fly and they urged us to empty our questioning and troublesome minds through meditation. I left the group and Guru Maharaj Ji married a tall California blonde. The deb stayed on for six more years until, according to newspaper accounts, she was kidnapped from an ashram in Jamaica by a "deprogrammer" hired by her wealthy family.

School held my attention, especially French—not that I was very good at it. "Baudelaire, qu'est-ce qu'il voulait dire dans ce poème? Y-a-t-il quelqu'un qui peut me répondre? Mademoiselle McDonald?" asked the professor. I let out a startled "Oui?" recognizing my name and the word "poème." "Comment avez-vous réagi à 'Spleen'?" Silence. "Oui?" "Avez-vous lu le poème, Mademoiselle McDonald?" I nodded yes. I *had* read the poem, and even liked it, once I'd looked up every other word in the dictionary. But in class my brain simply could not locate French words, nor could my mouth speak them. I was squirming. Monsieur Pamplume said something I didn't understand, and called on Gwen Pasteur, who'd been waving her hand the whole time. I smirked and pouted. If *I* had gone to high school in France, *I'd* be babbling about "*la tristesse*," too. She shouldn't even be in Beginning French! Monsieur Pamplume read the poem aloud, and I swooned to the music of his rich, resonant voice. "J'ai plus de souvenirs que si j'avais mille ans," he read, closing his eyes and releasing the words from his lips like a kiss. He never spoke English to the students, although it was rumored that he was fluent. I'd heard that he spent part of every year in India, which explained the Indian-style saffron robes he sometimes wore to class. It was heavenly when he read, his white-haired head bowed as if in prayer, his voice carrying so well the gorgeous cadence of the French language. More often than not, I didn't understand the words, but the sound entranced me.

The hardest part of college was its interruption by holidays and summer vacations. As much as I looked forward to seeing my family, I resisted going home. The projects were becoming more drug-infested and unsafe, and I no longer had any close friends there. Most of the children with whom I had played marbles and shared secrets were now troubled adults who looked only vaguely familiar. So, more than once, I opted to stay on campus over the summer and work with the dorm-cleaning crew. Friends didn't mince words. "Are you sick? I can't wait to get home." I could.

This time, I emerged from freshman year with respectable grades. Emboldened, I decided during sophomore year to apply for the Junior Year Abroad in France program. I'd only been out of the Northeast a couple of times and had never ventured outside the country. But everyone else was doing it and surviving: Judy was always in and out of India, as was Monsieur Pamplume; Laura had left her home in England for the United States; many of my friends had already been abroad. I don't know what exactly motivated my decision to go to France. Maybe the music of Monsieur Pamplume's readings, or my own wish to fly even higher and farther from the projects, or merely a collegian's wanderlust. Whatever the reason, I devised a foolproof plan to ensure acceptance into the program: I would declare French literature my major, and switch to something more practical when I returned from France. When I told friends I'd chosen French, they reacted as though I'd announced my intention to major in origami. "What are you going to do with *French?*" My parents' reactions reflected their respective travel experience. Daddy, who had been stationed in the South Pacific during World War II, was all for my trip. Mother's horizons reached to Alabama and back; thus she resigned herself to the idea with a "Lord have mercy!"

Waiting at JFK Airport in my fashion-don't polyester pantsuit and mustard-colored shoes, I certainly didn't *look* like I was en route to the world's fashion capital. I didn't even know at the time that Paris *was* a fashion capital. Most of the family was there to see me off. Luke carried my suitcases and avoided eye contact with Daddy. Alabama had not brought about the changes my father wished for, and his unwillingness to accept Luke "as is" was fatal to their relationship. After Alabama, Luke did a stint in the navy (a slap in the face of our pro-army father), moved to an apartment in Greenwich Village, and settled into his life-style, even taking part in the historic pro-gay Stonewall riots on Christopher Street. Unbeknownst to Daddy, Mother often had me attend the annual Gay Pride march to show family support for her "first baby." Now he lugged the heaviest suitcase, as if trying to prove something to Daddy. Ann concentrated on teasing me. She warned me against wearing shorts lest some hungry Frenchy mistake my limbs for frogs' legs. She was also living on her own, juggling dope, food stamps, eviction notices, and a newborn. Victor's army duty and Jean's family obligations kept them both away. Kevin didn't let go of my hand until the last minute. When the moment came for me to join the others, the family gathered around, embracing me one at a time. Mother said the usual things about eating enough and writing every once in a while. She had me verify for the umpteenth time the location of my brand-new passport. Daddy slipped two twenty-dollar bills into my hand.

The year-abroad program drew students from across the country. Of the eighty participants, four of us were black. There was a curly-haired guy who was nice but distant, a strange introvert from Texas wearing thick, chipped glasses, and Nikki Jones. Nikki was a Yalie from St. Louis who amply made up for the limitations of the other two. She was larger than life in every way, beginning with her solid six-foot body. Graced with a shrewd wit, a clever tongue, and a sailor's colorful vocabulary, Nikki took the world by its axis and bent it to her will. We were both August babies and bonded astrologically, in true college-girl style. She was incontestably the mighty Leo, and I the shrinking one. It was flattering that she befriended me, the "least freaked out," she said, of the black students. There were obviously no project people in the group, but looking around, I decided *black* would do just fine.

At Orly Airport I quickly concluded that *American* would also do just fine. Hundreds of Monsieur Pamplumes and Madame Guerriers scurried to and fro. The French looked very petite to us. Their small stature inspired dumb jokes about baguette-wielding Lilliputians. Next to the French, Nikki looked like a giant, and I seemed statuesque. My reading comprehension and writing ability were adequate, but understanding spoken French was quite another matter. Rapid-fire French words whizzed past my ears, indistinguishable from other airport noises. Speaking was going to be out of the question; after the first "boneshoor," I dared say nothing more. As a French major, I was at least a step ahead of my peers who had selected more practical studies like economics and pre-law. Nikki was a political-science major, in France to study at the prestigious Ecole des Sciences Politiques. I questioned whether her level of French would prove adequate to get her through the year.

Various living arrangements were available to us. There were aging French widows willing to house an American or two in return for a generous stipend, families with children eager to learn English, and private residences for French girls from bourgeois families. Nikki was going to a widow's *pension*, and I'd been assigned to the Foyer Jeanne d'Arc in the Montparnasse area. Managed by three nuns, the *foyer* accepted no more than four American girls, out of the fifty residents. Sister Paule had told the program director that American girls had a wild streak and she couldn't have too many running amok in the *foyer*. I was jetlagged and disoriented when I arrived at the residence. A nun in full habit greeted me at the door and showed me to my room. I crawled into bed and sank into a deep sleep. The following morning I was startled by the sight in the mirror. French mosquitoes had indulged in a full-course picnic on my face. I counted fifty bites. At breakfast, Sister Paule gasped, "Zut! Mon Dieu!" I laughed, surprised to hear a real French person use that expression. Nikki later said, "When I saw you with all those bumps on your face, I said to myself, shit, I hope that's not some kind of disease black people get when they come to France!"

The long French windows of my room opened onto a small courtyard with a statue of Joan of Arc in the center. Residence rules were strict: we showered between certain limited hours, received visitors exclusively in the very public glass visiting room, and were subject to an 11 p.m. curfew. We had meals in a sprawling refectory, where the din of metal chairs, clinking cutlery, and high-pitched French voices made my ears ring. The French girls wore tight slacks, leather boots, and makeup. I wore loose jeans, T-shirts, and sneakers. They chain-smoked cigarettes at open windows when the nuns weren't around, and were aloof, almost unfriendly. French clannishness drove me to seek out Americans, and I became friends with Jeannie, a minister's daughter from the Midwest who was a dance major. Sitting together at meals, we commiserated about our weak language skills and haughty hosts. Poor Jeannie—she heard one too many of my stories about hiding boxes of pistachio nuts in my waistband in supermarkets. "If something is overpriced, it's not really stealing, because overpricing itself is a form of theft," I argued. The day of that discourse, Jeannie burst into my room, red-nosed and frantic. "I got caught! It was awful." She had slipped one little tube of mascara in her purse. The store detective took all the money she had, an amount far greater than the cost of the item, and let her go with a warning. She had never before attempted shoplifting. "At least he let you go," I said, inwardly tickled by what had happened. "But I'm the daughter of a minister! My dad would die!" Our friendship survived my bad advice and shored up our spirits but did nothing for our French language skills.

In France, I was liberated from the Vassar girl/project girl conflict. No one judged me on specifics, and I had nothing to prove. The French saw me as just another American, though I didn't see myself that way at all. I viewed Americans as white patriots in "Love it or Leave it" T-shirts, with a flag on their lawns, who didn't want me in school with their children. I was black, period. The French drew no such distinctions, which meant I no longer had to worry about making *African Americans* look good. Or bad. Whatever I did was attributed to Americanness, not blackness. What a switch—a black person with the power to make white people look bad. Given how negatively the American media routinely portrayed us, I was tempted. School began in October. I took language classes with foreigners at the Alliance Française and literature courses with the French at the Sorbonne. The French system of instruction seemed rigid and formal after the fluidity of

Vassar. At the Sorbonne, a professor lectured at a podium while students feverishly took notes. No first names, no class participation, no give-and-take. The weekly discussion groups held in smaller classrooms were slightly more relaxed, but I found the Gauloise-laden air toxic.

I enjoyed moving about in a big city, and the bustle and energy of Paris reminded me of Manhattan. The similarity stopped there. The beauty of the City of Light's gently curved wrought-iron balconies and sculpture-studded gardens far surpassed New York's glass-and-steel chaos. Over time, I began feeling more comfortable exploring my own and nearby arrondissements but didn't dare venture much farther for fear of encounters of the French kind. Such as the newspaper vendor who flew into a rage when I politely asked directions. All I understood from the stream of invective he spewed my way was: "They come here and can't even speak the language." Or the charming *patissière* who tried to sell me seven croissants when I'd only asked for one. She wrapped one as I was pulling out my francs. Then she wrapped another, and then another. "Non, non! Un! Un suhl!" She sneered, "Vous avez dit sept, mademoiselle!" then mumbled to herself, "Ah, mais ça, alors . . . ça c'est chiant." Exuding contempt as only the French can, she shoved one croissant across the counter and overcharged me.

Rather than interact with the French, I preferred wandering the wide shaded walkways of the Luxembourg Gardens, following the narrow streets of the Latin Quarter, and climbing the stone steps inside Notre Dame to take in, alongside ancient gargoyles, the low aerial view of Paris.

After classes, we did the French thing and hung out in cafés over cups of *chocolat chaud* and *croque monsieur* sandwiches. Before departing New York, the program director lectured us about our status as "honorary ambassadors of goodwill for the United States." She had the wrong diplomats. Our gang was always true to stereotype: haughty Americans with appalling accents and boisterous behavior. Outlandish in purple plastic sunglasses and her grand-mother's fake fur, Nikki was a scourge on the French, and the rest of us loved her for it. "Garçon! Garçon!" she commanded, waving impatiently. "Doo chocolaz, see voo pleeze." Her French accent usually evoked a look of incomprehension in the *garçon* ranks. "The French are so backwards—they don't even understand their own language! Doo, misshur, doo. Comprende? Un, doo, twa? *Doo.*" Exasperated, she'd hold up two fingers. She forbade tipping. "Don't leave that bastard anything. Look how long it took us to get service. He sees niggers sitting at a table and walks the other way. Tip, my ass!"

Travel was rarely without incident. If Nikki was sitting in their special designated area, the elderly, disabled, and war veterans would just have to stand. "My ancestors already made the necessary sacrifices," she said. She was fearless, daring even to tangle with that most daunting class of Parisians: old Frenchwomen. One el-derly madame made the mistake of snarling when Nikki refused to give up her seat on a crowded bus. Hunched under a black shawl, the woman let loose a flood of French insults. Nikki was non-plussed. "Do you be-*lieve* this shit! She's gonna *make* me get up and give her my seat. *Madame*, you need to take your *derrière* else-where, and *vite!*" They stared each other down, Nikki seated, ma-dame standing, until our stop arrived. The cantankerous old Frenchwoman was a sacrificial lamb made to pay for all the daily slights and insults inflicted on American students. Our friends cheered Nikki's American diplomacy. As for school, Nikki was notorious, a wild woman among hardworking drones. Despite cut-ting classes whenever she wanted and taking off a month to spend with her boyfriend, she aced her "Sciences Po" exams, graduated from Yale, earned a Master's at Johns Hopkins, and became a banker.

I also met Francesca, the daughter of an Egyptian father and an Italian mother, who had been raised in upper-class London. Francesca resembled a light-skinned black American and was tormented by her yearning to have blond hair and blue eyes. "All the boys I liked in boarding school preferred the blond girls," Francesca complained in her very English accent. "I wish they could see that inside I *am* a blue-eyed blonde." I knew few mixed-race people and was moved by her candor and obvious suffering. My sympathetic words failed to console, however, and Francesca agonized all year about her "cruel fate."

She was much more helpful to me than I was to her. Her father had come to Paris on business and wanted to take Francesca and a couple of her friends to dinner. I panicked when she invited me. The only "restaurants" I'd been in up to that point were pizza shops and Chinese fast-food places. A wealthy businessman, Mr. Rahkla had made reservations in a fancy seventh arrondissement restaurant. "Suppose I mess up," I asked, "or use the wrong silverware?" "Just do everything I do," she said. At dinner, I concentrated on Francesca's every move as she worked her way from the outside in, through a row of shiny cutlery. Intimidated by everything, from the way the *garçon* leaned toward me to take my order to the enormous cloth napkin bunched up on my lap, I participated little in the conversation. But other than momentarily forgetting myself and asking in English, "Do you have soda?" I did all right that evening, although I barely remember the food. Francesca's simple lesson would serve me well years later as I made the rounds, as a Paris resident, of innumerable French restaurants, fancy and otherwise.

Winter brought gray clouds and wrapped the city in cold. It took that long for me to learn, after being scolded in first class by a métro agent glaring at my second-class ticket, that there were two classes in the Paris subway cars. And that, no matter how hard you stared, the car door would not open automatically. Language progress was just as slow. I had made some improvement, but my questionable grammar, child's vocabulary, and ringing American accent still caused the natives to flinch. My American friends were fun, but they weren't going to help me learn to speak French. Only the French could do that, but the French girls in the *foyer* limited conversation to a polite *"Bonjour"* as they rushed down the corridor. I had the impression that we *américaines* were considered vaguely corrupt and certainly corrupting, a little too independent and tomboyish by French standards of femininity. Or maybe they avoided us because struggling through the awful noise of our butchered French was simply too painful. For whatever reason, by the end of the year not one of the four Americans living in the residence had developed a friendship with a French European. Francophones who were not European were much more open.

At dinner one evening, I glimpsed the top of a tall Afro leaving the refectory. I didn't know there were any other black people in the residence and was intrigued by the dark-skinned young woman retreating with a tray of food. The next time I saw her slipping out with her dinner, I said *"Bonsoir."* Her friendliness surprised me; she invited me to drop by her room anytime. Her name was packed with syllables—Myrianne Montlouis-Calixte—and she was from Martinique, a place I hadn't heard of, and was in Paris studying math. She spoke almost no English and my French was in its infancy, but we managed to communicate. Appearances notwithstanding, Myrianne wasn't antisocial, just anti-French. She found Parisians as cold and gray as the city, and missed her island home.

Through my new friend, I discovered an entire community of *antillaises* from the West Indian bourgeoisie tucked away in the residence and was invited to some of their social gatherings outside the *foyer*. These girls from Guadeloupe and Martinique ate alone, or in each other's rooms. They were elated to meet an African American and bombarded me with questions about racism, Harlem, black entertainers, and anything that touched upon the lives of black people in "America." They giggled at my French and laughed outright when I attempted to explain that I was black, not American. "Mais, Jeannette, you are so ver-ry américaine," said Marie, who spoke a little English. She said I looked American, dressed American, and walked like an American.

I was curious about their hostile attitude toward the Paris-born *antillaise*, who took her meals with French friends and described herself as "*française*." They said the French didn't accept them as equals; therefore, French West Indians should refuse to claim a French identity. Even more annoying to them was Binta, a twenty-year-old Senegalese married to a much older French businessman. The relationship incensed the West Indians, and the framed photo of her husband Binta kept on a bedside nightstand did little to improve her standing. Binta certainly was a special case. Just before my return to the United States, she begged me to send her some American skin-lightening cream. "I want to be light-skinned and beautiful like Diana Ross and Donna Summer." These and other cross-cultural friendships were eye-opening: while African Americans continued to reel from the destructive legacy of slavery and racism, people of color worldwide struggled with their own forms of racial turmoil. I realized that the social and psychological effects of racism transcended national borders. Other friends I made that year were equally fascinating. Much of my time was spent with Linda and Ernie, Indonesian twins who were classically trained pianists. The three of us had long conversations in each other's rooms and were sometimes joined by Ike, also Indonesian. Ike's father had named her after his hero, President Eisenhower. I was also very close to Wisdom, a gorgeous African from Togo whose dream in life was to move to Colorado and "live like an American." His father had given Wisdom's four brothers names that were just as remarkable: Peace, Light, Love, and Might. There were times in Paris when I felt as if my brain could barely process the wealth of new impressions, surprising names, and puzzling accents.

During spring break I traveled to the walled town of St.-Malo in Brittany. I explored the ramparts, cruised around on a rented *mobylette* pretending to be a member of Hell's Angels, and, at low tide, ventured out by foot to Grand Bé Island to visit the tomb of Chateaubriand. By year's end, I had visited Martinique, fallen in love with French literature, and read everything available on the experiences of African Americans in Paris; no one claimed France was perfect, but many African Americans saw it as a haven from racism. My greatest accomplishment, however, was that I had learned to speak good French, which couldn't be said for the American students who had continued through the year to huddle together in cafés.

Senior year, I returned to Vassar with a stack of French records and an obsession with Paris. I'd also fallen head over heels for a teenager from Martinique, but the long-distance relationship didn't survive the voyage across the Atlantic. I kept French as my major, and the year passed in a flurry of term papers, thesis research, and preparations for graduation. Unable to come up with a feasible plan for my future, I applied to graduate school in French literature as well as to law school, in the hope that fate would make the decision I couldn't. No such luck. I was admitted to both. Unable to decide one way or the other, I enrolled in an NYU Master's-degree program in France and deferred admission to Cornell Law School until the following September. All I wanted was more of Paris; real life, with its dreary careerism, could wait a year.

Graduation day sparkled with flashbulbs and grins. The French Department gave me an achievement award. Ernest had also successfully completed four years—in prison—and had been paroled; we posed for photos and called ourselves "The Graduates." I was a project girl *and* a Vassar girl now, and glad to be both. A bright sun slowly crossed campus, pulling with it light and shadow, just as I had done.

PART 2

Daddy lived just long enough to see me grab hold of "the ticket" he so revered. The year after I graduated from Vassar, he suffered a fatal heart attack at the age of fifty-four. I was back in France studying French literature and living in the Fondation des Etats-Unis dorm of Cité Universitaire. During much of December I had been troubled by dreams in which the whole family was crying; in one dream I saw, for the first time, Ernest crying. I had also been bothered by painful sensations in my left arm. And I was inexplicably distracted, then possessed, and eventually overcome by one dominant feeling: that I should go home for the holidays. Not a welcome thought, as I'd already planned to spend Christmas in Paris. The pull was so insistent that on Christmas Eve I found myself standing with my suitcase at the McDonalds' door. I hadn't told anyone I was coming, and in my leather boots, tight corduroy jeans, and slanted beret, I was unrecognizable. Almost. My knock brought Mother to the peephole. "Oh, my Jesus! Lord have mercy, let me get this door unlocked! Kevin, your sister's at the door!" Daddy died suddenly five days later. I was stunned when Mother said he'd been having pains in his left arm.

I have no doubt that he had called me to his side that Christmas. Our relationship had been complex—never openly conflictual, but not easy either. I admired and resented his high-pressure aspirations for us. Of all the children, I think I had taken his maxims and dreams most to heart, and in a sense had suffered as a result. Yet I was grateful that he pushed me so, and now attribute much of my achievement to him. Sometimes the more difficult bonds grow into the strongest—ours was one of those.

His funeral drew old and new family friends from all over the projects, along with post-office co-workers and relatives from elsewhere. The twins he'd saved from the fire, now young men, stared into the casket and shook their heads slowly. Luke sat with Mother, who looked lost, and Ann, who was in dark sunglasses. Victor, now a sergeant, had come from Germany and was still in uniform. He paired off with his buddy Jean, who kept an eye on Ann's girls and her own. Kevin's knees gave way as we stood together at Daddy's open casket, but I held him up. And for the first time, I saw Ernest cry.

I waited alone at JFK for my return flight to Paris. I thought about the man who never really stopped being my Superman. The world felt less safe to me without him. And less amusing: I thought of the time he recorded Mother snoring to prove she did, and how he tried to learn Spanish in his sleep by playing language tapes under his pillow, and all the times he blasted our "uncultured" neighbors with cloying pseudoclassical music. He could also be overbearing and cruel; he'd finally come around concerning Luke's sexuality and had given him the you're-still-my-son talk, perhaps a little too late. There was so much to him that in a sense each of us had a different father. When I was a little girl, *my* father would wash dishes for me when it was my turn and I was too sleepy. And it was he who comforted me the afternoon I lay in bed after losing the sixth-grade spelling bee. *He* was the father *I'd* miss, the one I cried over through the interminable flight back.

In Paris I immersed myself in the intriguing people and enveloping charm of this city said to be of light, a place that seemed to harvest a much-needed lightness in me. I dropped out of the graduate program, reconnected with my *antillaise* friends and the three African Americans in the Fondation. The West Indians socialized at dinners lively with laughter, reggae, and excited talk about "back home." Politics and talk of *les français* inflamed tempers. My ears strained to recognize the French words and abandoned all effort when the conversation turned creole. I discovered blood sausages and sweet rum punch and danced in the Latin Quarter at the Black Sugar Club. Unabashed tourism appealed to my stateside compatriots, and together we strolled the boulevards and quays of the Latin Quarter and picnicked at the foot of the grandiose Place St.-Michel fountain. At the City of Science and Industry complex we gawked at the Géode, a massive shining steel globe mirrored in a sheet of water, and flocked to the Ile St.-Louis, home to splendid seventeenth-century houses set inside courtyards behind immense paneled doors. The city's many student discounts made it possible for us to visit museums and concerts and enjoy cheap meals in student canteens. I was enamored of Paris, but far from happy. The flowers of spring enlivened the city's look and summer warmed the air, but the months had done little to wash away my underlying grief.

I had put off law school for a year. Now the admissions office wanted to know if I still intended to enroll. The only lawyer I knew was the television character Perry Mason. But what else was there for a twenty-five-year-old to do? I had to face employers' demands for marketable skills, and all I had was a college degree in French literature—only theoretically a skill, and hardly marketable. Moreover, Mother said Daddy would want me to go. All indicators pointed to Ithaca.

The university had a wide mix of graduate schools, including engineering, medical, and the state-financed Agricultural School. Urban through and through, I couldn't fathom what could possibly be taught at the "Ag" school, which some students maliciously claimed recruited inbreds and rednecks off farms. The law school, in contrast, was a private institution. Its classrooms, law-student dormitory, library, and squash courts were all in one building, Hughes Hall, a concentration I cherished when the below-zero temperatures of winter hit upstate New York. The sprawling campus was densely wooded in some places and seemed ten times the size of Vassar. I had grown up feeling there was safety in numbers—of people, not trees—and stuck close to the law school.

I wasn't prepared for the resentment other students sometimes showed toward future lawyers. A gravel path separated the law school up the hill from the undergraduate residences below. I became familiar with the voice of the undergrad who always shouted from the path, "I'd rather be an asshole than a law student!" His words didn't make me feel any better about my haphazard decision.

Of the five hundred law students, the dozen black students quickly found each other. The older ones gave us new recruits all manner of advice, ranging from little-known sources of financial aid to the importance of getting on staff at a student-published legal journal. If you didn't qualify automatically through top grades, your best bet was to come to school a few weeks before the beginning of fall classes and enter the writing competition. Determined to shine, I resolved to do just that.

I got on especially well with Charles, a fellow Brooklynite in his second year who wore professorial wire-rimmed glasses, played the organ in church, and was a tireless disco dancer. He helped me get my bearings, recommending useful study aids and suggesting which professors to avoid. He's now a law professor himself. Beth, a native of upper-middle-class Boston, also became a good friend, despite our different backgrounds, differences I had learned to expect at such schools. Her genuineness and irreverent sense of humor were a welcome relief from the haughty pomposity of most everyone else.

Compared to the passion of French literature and the magic of Paris, law instruction felt boring and life in Hughes Hall barren. The only excitement of the year was when I impetuously flew to Paris in the middle of exam period to revive my love affair with the Martiniquan, now an adult. It didn't work. I returned to school with nothing but a poignant story for my teacher about rushing to the side of a sick sister. Grudgingly, he permitted me to take the exam I missed, "only because of the exceptional circumstances."

I completed the first year, but my unimpressive grades reflected my lack of interest in law studies. Nonetheless, I was fortunate enough to find a summer job in Manhattan as a government-agency legal intern. There I met a young civil-rights lawyer who had the same name as a well-known congresswoman famous for hats. "Abzug? So where's your hat?" I'd smirked, reading the nameplate on her desk. "Janet! That's my *mother* you're talking about." I thought she was joking. We grew to be very close and I eventually met her famous mother and she my unknown one. Liz had the intensity of a solid rocket booster and the competitiveness of a race-car driver. When we ran in the annual summer Corporate Challenge, I had the distinct feeling that all she wanted was to cross the finish line before *me*, which she did. She took a mentor's interest in my career, helping with my brief-writing and giving advice, right down to the brand of underwear, on exactly what style of clothing befitted a woman lawyer. At the end of August I went up to school early, as planned, to compete for a slot at one of the journals.

Classes hadn't yet started and few students were on Cornell's campus when I showed up to begin my second year. First-year law students were the only ones allowed to live in Hughes Hall, so I took a room in a nearby dorm. At the law school, I picked up the competition research package, loaded with photocopied cases, articles, and statutes, all of which I was to analyze and fashion into a persuasively written legal brief. I'd be chosen to join a journal if mine was better than most.

One evening I stepped from the dorm elevator and saw a stranger standing at my door. I didn't know him, although I had noticed him in the lobby when I moved in. He looked older than most of the students, even those in graduate school. In fact, he was a lot older than the rest of us, having just been paroled from a lengthy prison stay, during which he'd taken college-level courses. School administrators were aware of his criminal background but had admitted him nonetheless under an affirmative-action program for "special" students. I knew none of this as I approached my room, and assumed the man was just another student. "Yes?" He introduced himself and invited me out for a drink. I said I didn't drink. "How about some milk, then?" "Water?" "Ice cream?" I had spent the whole day in the library and was tired. I said no, thanks, and unlocked my door, adding that I was sure he'd be able to find someone else to go out for ice cream. His manner changed abruptly and he became tense and hostile. I heard him say something about black women being all the same. Then he said, "If you know so much, do you know you're gonna get raped tonight?"

The glue holding me together dissolved in my shock. It was as though time and place ruptured, and I plunged into a swirl of what shrinks called neurotic episodes. The man left me crazy, my head unhinged like a kicked-in door. He was immediately apprehended and locked up in jail. I was locked away in the hospital for the night. A nurse gave me ten days' worth of antibiotics to kill off the venereal disease he'd left behind. The police came back the next morning and said, "You can go back to your dorm room now. He's in custody. You're safe." Of course, I wasn't safe, and would never be again. A couple of friends accompanied me to my room—I wouldn't go alone. A stain on the bedspread sent a shudder through me. I tore the bedspread from the bed and stuffed it in a ball in the closet. I couldn't tolerate being in the room and was allowed to move back into Hughes Hall. Beth spent time listening and trying to comfort me, as did

Charles, but I was inconsolable. There weren't enough hours in the day to fill with tears, nor hours in the night to hold all my nightmares. Classes began without me. I wanted to go, to keep up with the others, but couldn't move from my bed. My therapist at the local counseling center was also overwhelmed by depression—mine. She called me up a few weeks after I began seeing her. "It's Edith. From the counseling center. I can't see you anymore. You remind me too much of my suicidal husband, and I find myself constantly worrying about you. I'm sorry." I told her I understood and asked hopefully what finally happened with her husband. "He committed suicide."

I was so angry I wanted to kill someone, anyone. The nearest person was me. Why had I failed to protect myself? Why had I no gun when I needed one? Or a black belt in karate? The rape was my fault, and unconsciously, or perhaps not, I set out to punish myself. Initially, I could get sedatives from the school nurse. But that ended the third time I was half carried into the infirmary after washing down as many pills with as much alcohol as my stomach could hold. But there was still beer. I'd chug a quart or two and stagger through the halls of the dorm. Friends pleaded with me to pull myself together, to go to class, put it behind me. I resented their reference to "it." There was no "it," there was me, devastated. How would I put *me* behind me? I felt them growing bored with my relentless pain; I saw reproach in their eyes as they sat with me in my airless room, their eyes glancing at watches, seeking book titles, involuntarily looking toward passersby on the path. They didn't want to hear me describe the cut over his eye or his partially severed finger or the violent flare of his nostrils as he threatened to beat me unconscious if I screamed. No, they'd heard enough of all that. In a way, their waning interest didn't really matter. Concern, or its absence, changed nothing.

Professor Younger visited. Judith, not Irving, her more well-known husband. She taught Property. I had never participated in class discussions because I understood nothing she said. But I did raise my hand, and was the only one to do so, when she asked if anyone *didn't* know what a mortgage was. I guess that was how she remembered who I was. No other faculty or administrator deemed such a visit appropriate, and hers was a real surprise. Her large eyes brimmed with compassion as we attempted conversation. Silence filled much of the visit, but her presence was more of a comfort than any words could have been.

I accepted an invitation from some friends to go to a downtown diner. We all hoped it would give me momentary respite from my deepening crisis. In the middle of the meal, I excused myself and walked over to a pay phone. "Hello, 911? Send someone to the Ithaca Diner. I think I'm going to kill myself." I returned to the table and took my seat in silence. Within minutes, two policemen appeared in the diner. I stood up and was escorted away as a table of law-school friends looked on in bewilderment.

I asked to be taken to the on-campus infirmary, and curled up in the back seat of the patrol car, where I fell asleep. The sound of tires on gravel awakened me as the car came to a stop. The cops walked me into a building that I didn't recognize, exchanged a few whispered words with an attendant, and left me standing there, at a state psychiatric hospital that was many miles from Cornell. No sooner was I inside than I regretted making the call. Slow-moving figures shuffled around in tattered, flimsy gowns, obviously hospitalized for the long haul. I, on the other hand, was processed during intake as a "voluntary admit"—the only nut who had *asked* to be locked up in this medieval asylum. In my cell-like room I lay down on the thin mattress and stared at the doughnut-sized hole in the door. An eye looked back at me through the opening.

The clamor of morning woke me to the full horror of my situation. Patients were lining up single-file to receive their meds—drugs I was relieved to learn I wouldn't have to take. One by one they approached the attendant, mouths gaping open, to receive the pills that would ensure their continued torpor. I wanted out. Immediately. "Excuse me, when can I leave?" I was told it would be a couple of days, that I must first be "interviewed" by the psychiatrist, who came in once a week from his private practice. The maximum stay of a voluntary admission was normally three days, she said, unless, of course, the interview indicated otherwise. Her indifferent air depressed me even more. Couldn't she see I was different from the others? Why hadn't those cops taken me to the infirmary as I'd asked? Seventy-two long hours stretched before me, and already the first one was unendurable.

The day room was the place everyone was forced to go during waking hours. Spending the day alone in one's room, the only thing I wanted to do, was unacceptable antisocial behavior. I ventured inside. There were garish flowered curtains and a brown sloping sofa strewn with lint. Magazines with ripped covers and bent *Reader's Digests* competed for floor space with building blocks, hospital slippers, and torn bits of cloth. An old-fashioned record player, its empty turntable spinning in silence, finished the dismal tableau. Green-gowned patients slumped, paced, or simply stared into space. Everyone was white, not surprising in a small town like Ithaca. In any case, at such levels of disorientation, race mattered little to any of us.

The third day arrived; I have little memory of how the other two passed. "The doctor can see you now, Miss McDonald." The narrow office held a metal desk, several stacks of books, and the visiting shrink's hefty frame, resplendent in jeweled cuff links, a bracelet, and a pinkie ring, all gold. He asked questions about my background and family history, and why I'd made the emergency call. I was determined to give the right answer, the one that would get me out. "Oh, I was just a little depressed. I overreacted to . . . what happened." "You mean the . . ." "Yes," I quickly interrupted, not wanting to hear him say the word. "I've put it behind me and am eager to get back to school and pick up where I left off." He smiled. "Very good, my friend. I think you can be discharged." In a flash I was packed and sitting on the sofa, unnoticed by the patients and ignored by the attendants.

Charles rushed in. I looked at him in shock, wondering how he knew where to find me. Having unsuccessfully tried to get a ride from friends, I had been waiting for someone from the prosecutor's office to pick me up. "Come on, Janet," he said angrily, scanning the room. "You don't belong here." I took a last look at the patients, present only physically. There was no one to say goodbye to.

I went back to school but avoided classes. *It* blotted out everything else from my mind: the parole-revocation hearing scheduled for the rapist. I dreaded testifying for many reasons, the primary one being that the parolee had the right to be present. A young police detective met with me to explain why I had to. "If you wanna keep this guy behind bars until trial, you're gonna have to testify at the hearing." Pause. "Otherwise, it could be unsafe for you. It's as simple as that."

The hearing room felt much too small for the judge, the detective, and the rapist, seated just inches away from me. I was struck by the fact that we were all black. The rapist lied calmly about what he'd done. Then the judge, who'd flown in from New York City on the red-eye, asked for my "version." I saw him stifle a yawn as I spoke. The hearing ended. Several days later, the detective phoned me and happily announced that parole had been revoked and that I'd be receiving a copy of the decision. He prepared me for the "unfortunate" wording—the basis for revocation was possession of a controlled substance, one joint. The judge made no mention of me, he said. "Don't feel bad. He's in the middle of a divorce and hates women right now." The detective hesitated—there was something else. "This may not be the best time, but if you ever want to get together, you know, to talk, maybe take in a movie . . ." I was dumbfounded. No, I said, it wasn't the best time.

The hearing over, I turned my anguished attention toward the next ordeal—the trial. What would they ask me? Would I be able to hold up? Would anyone believe his lies? Rarely did I leave my dorm room. There was no longer any circadian rhythm to my day; night followed night. I was no longer a law student but a dorm hermit. Toward October, school officials began to urge me to go home, each nudge a little more insistent. I hadn't yet told anyone in the family what had happened to me, unwilling to give voice to words so humiliating. Eventually, I had no alternative but to tell Mother, since I had at last agreed to leave school. I told her on the telephone. She sighed long and deep. We never mentioned *it* again.

New York became a city of mirrors where everywhere I saw his reflection in the eyes of mean, angry men sizing me up for the kill. I found a job as a paralegal at a Wall Street law firm. Liz helped me find a therapist and told me about a freelance photographer named Donna who was looking for a roommate to share her seven-room apartment on Eastern Parkway. I moved in and found her to be just what the doctor ordered. She said rapists should be tortured slowly and then castrated. Her fierce views validated my growing rage. I likened myself to a Wagnerian Valkyrie, a warrior. I began carrying a knife at all times, kept a club under my mattress, and succeeded in buying a gun. New York can feel scary even at the best of times, and now the very air was heavy with threat. I wanted more than to protect myself—I wanted to kill. My naturally soft voice and polite, well-educated manner allowed me to browse in the library at work, ask police officers for directions, and pass through the general population, with a fully loaded .38 strapped into a cloth holster under my pin-striped blouse.

The rape case was set for trial. In the time leading up to the late-March trial date, I so convinced my worried therapist I'd murder the rapist on the spot if I thought he'd be acquitted that two days before trial she terminated therapy in a panic. "I can't work with you, Janet. I'm pro-life and you're pro-death." Perhaps, but she certainly wasn't pro-fessional, and with Donna's help I filed a complaint against her for professional misconduct. I was on the warpath.

Alone, I flew back to Ithaca to testify. "Do you swear to tell the whole truth?" I swear and I do. The rapist swears and he doesn't. The prosecutor seeks to introduce evidence about the defendant's lengthy criminal record. His white-haired lawyer, who plans to retire to Florida after this case, jumps to his feet. The judge rules that details of prior convictions are irrelevant and of prior rapes prejudicial. I learn that the defendant is also from a New York public housing project. The memory of Olga López flashes in my mind. I glance his way. His eyes stare me down as if planting an unspoken hex. My water-filled paper cup shakes as I take a sip. I am a knot inside. "Isn't it a fact that you had to be put in the school infirmary for abusing pills and alcohol?" I try to explain but the lawyer mocks my answer and moves to the next question on his list. "Now, if I could direct your attention to the night of the so-called rape. Were you on drugs and alcohol then?" The defendant's laugh precedes the prosecutor's, "Objection, your Honor!" The judge overrules the district attorney and instructs me to answer. "No." "Now, you're from New York, aren't you? Yet, all of a sudden, you don't know how to deal with a man in your room?" He directs his sarcastic voice to the men and women of the jury and doesn't seem to mind that the inevitable objection is sustained. He forges ahead. "Now, Miss McDonald, you were recently committed to a state hospital because of emotional problems, isn't that true?"

I am both absent and present. I know I've been crying because the district attorney hands me a tissue, his eyes on the jury. It shouldn't, but the defense lawyer's attitude hurts me. Mostly because I'm convinced he knows his client is guilty. "Vassar is a whole different world from the streets of Harlem where my client grew up, isn't it? And you felt a little superior to him, didn't you, and then ashamed after the two of you made love, so you decided to cry rape, isn't that what happened?" "Objection, badgering!" The rapist makes a loud snorting sound and rattles his leg irons; I look his way and my eyes are met with the same threatening glare. A teacher leads an assembly of white children into the room. They slide noisily onto benches. A civics class here to watch the criminal justice system in action. I try to concentrate on the tingling sensation in my feet. My legs go numb. The prosecutor, whom I think of as my attorney even though he isn't, is even more aggressive with the defendant, who takes the stand on the second day. Unfortunately, I don't get to see him cry. In fact, he remains smug and relaxed.

The lawyers are doing their summations. A bird alights on a ledge of the courtroom window. I hear: "Miss McDonald can't seem to tell the difference between romance and rape. What we have here are two college kids, both black I might add, feeling alienated and lonely. They meet, strike up a friendship, and hop in the sack. Happens every day, ladies and gentlemen." The lawyer glances victoriously in the direction of the small-town jury of farmers, supermarket clerks, and secretaries. The bird soars off. I, too, want to fly away.

Home, I talk only to Donna about the trial. A call comes from the prosecutor. "We won!" he cheers. Perhaps he had won, but to me the verdict is the very definition of a Pyrrhic victory. He adds that the defense lawyer plans to appeal. The hellish quality of my life doesn't leave as I return to its troubled rhythm. Six months later, I think I'm ready to go back to law school. I'm not.

Arson Suspected in Law School Dorm Fires

AP NEW YORK   Hayden Hall, the dormitory housing
New York University's law students, has been plagued by a
series of mysterious fires during the past two weeks, according
to a Fire Department spokesman. The fires involved rubbish
contained in trash bins and have caused the dorm to be evac-
uated several times. Angry students are demanding that the
administration do more to catch the arsonist, sources said.
Administration officials could not be reached for comment.
A source in the Fire Marshal's office said the investigation is
focusing on dorm residents and employees.

For weeks, there had been meetings among students, meetings
with administrators, meetings with campus security officials, and

still the fires continued. Here, there, in the afternoon, late at night, on the seventh floor, the third floor, the fourteenth floor. The scenario never varied. On each floor, the trash inside a metal bin in a concrete closet mysteriously catches fire. The small blazes cause a mighty commotion and students stumble down the stairwell and onto the street.

It was sometime around midnight when the peal of fire alarms startled me. I'd just come in and was lying on my bed, thinking. The metallic cry rattled my insides. I was sharing a room on the fourteenth floor of the Washington Square Park dorm with a first-year law student. The routine had become dreadfully familiar. I stood from my bed, Kim leapt out of hers, and we grabbed our coats to join the rush of students filing out of the building. Some of them were swearing, others laughing. But most just hurried in silence.

A fire truck swerved around the corner, flashing white and red lights. An army of firefighters in black gear tumbled from the front and back of the truck, and swarmed through the lobby and up the stairs. Outside, shouting students crowded around the law-school dean, who'd hastened to the scene from his apartment in a nearby high-rise. "What is the school doing?!" "Why are the fires still going on? If anything happens, NYU is strictly liable!" "We're paying a lot of money to live in this dorm and should have round-the-clock security patrols in the halls!" Dean Redlich looked slightly disoriented, like someone abruptly awakened from a heavy sleep. He raised his voice over the hubbub. "We are doing everything . . . Security patrols have been stepped up across campus . . . The fire marshals are conducting . . ." The clamor increased. Redlich raised his hands in the air. "Please! We must remain calm. Panicking isn't going to . . ." The students were in no mood to be calmed. "If this were happening in your building, you'd have caught the guy by now! You're safe, but what about us?" "Yeah!" I chimed in, looking him right in the eye with a reproachful frown.

It wasn't the first time I had come face to face with the dean. We had met months ago at a reception to welcome second-year transfer students to the law school. "And you are . . ." he'd said, smiling, a question in his voice. He stole a rapid glance at my stick-on name tag and we both said "Janet McDonald" at the same time. I smiled and gripped my ginger ale, concentrating on holding the paper napkin under the glass with my pinkie. I liked the bushy eyebrows over his intense, intelligent eyes. But I felt humiliated by his sympathy. He knows, I thought, and he feels sorry for me. I looked away and he said, "Well, very nice to meet you. You're from . . ." "Brooklyn," I offered, cringing for some reason. "Yes, that's right! Well, welcome to NYU. We're happy to have you." He didn't ask and I didn't tell, but we both knew. The heat in my ears spread to my face and I wanted to sob. We exchanged smiles—his friendly, mine pained—and he walked over to another student. Transferring from one law school to another isn't easy. There were only a half dozen of us and we formed an elite group. Few students even try, because of the stringent admission criteria. The successful applicant usually has straight A's and a compelling reason. I knew better than most which criterion carried more weight with admissions officers. Every other school had turned me down because of my unimpressive grades. NYU accepted me because of my compelling reason—the rape.

The university was grappling with a severe shortage of student housing, and the law-school dorm was no exception. Students from out of town were squeezed into whatever space was available. Rooms designed for one student often housed two, no reconstruction or remodeling necessary. Just a second single bed dragged in and left against a wall. Quarters that might feel spacious to lovers felt short on breathing room for two strangers. Most students, however, were simply grateful for a place to live on campus, given the exorbitant rents charged for apartments by the Washington Square area's major landlord—New York University.

I couldn't afford to stay in Donna's Eastern Parkway apartment, since I would no longer be working. That left the projects, but living at home wasn't an option. Mother's apartment had become a buzzing media center of droning televisions and blaring radios in every room—regardless of the presence or absence of viewers or listeners. But what I feared more than the noise was what or whom I might encounter on my daily subway rides. I completed the housing-request form without much hope, since my family lived right across the Brooklyn Bridge. But the word "projects" must have impressed the housing-office staff because my request was accorded the same priority as one from a resident of Wyoming. I was given dormitory housing along with all the other out-of-towners.

They say: Ask and ye shall receive. Even more attention should be given the companion axiom: Be careful what you ask for, you might get it. I was allotted a single room on the fourteenth floor of Hayden Hall. And so was Kim Yoo, a new student fresh from Princeton University. The same room. "Hi. I'm from Princeton, New Jersey. It's one of the wealthiest suburbs in the country." She told me about her long-haired boyfriend and said they called themselves John and Yoko. She confided that she thought black guys looked kind of "doofy" because of their "big feet," and found it ironic that we were roommates. "My parents would never let you in our house, even though you went to Vassar. They're afraid of black people. Most Koreans are." But Kim wasn't afraid of me. At least, not then.

Standing that night against a backdrop of fire trucks and angry law students, Dean Redlich looked very different from the person I'd met at the reception. His face was pale and more lined, and his furrowed forehead showed worry. Plaid pajamas were visible from beneath his long winter coat. Up on the fourteenth floor, a mess of dripping, blackened trash smoldered in a metal bin. "You can go back in now!" shouted a firefighter. Animated conversations competed with elevator sounds as we regained our rooms and settled in for a night of troubled sleep.

The next day's lunchtime talk centered on the most recent blaze. I was in the student lounge with a couple of classmates. We dropped our books at the nearest available table and headed over to the sandwich counter. Yoshi was adamant, her voice rising above the din. She was responding to the suggestion that someone on the domestic staff might be setting the fires. "No way it's one of the workers! Why would they want to burn down the dorm? I've come up with the profile. It's definitely a guy. White. A WASP. Probably from a wealthy family. The father's a successful lawyer and Junior just got rejected by *Law Review*. Unable to handle failure, he's cracking." Yoshi Wasaki was a star third-year and had been given a staff position on the prestigious student journal to which she was referring. Upon arriving at NYU, I had again entered the journal's writing competition, but was not selected. All the major Manhattan law firms were courting her, as were many out-of-state employers. Although of two minds about the whole corporate-law-firm scene, I was nevertheless plagued by envy.

Pleased with her analysis, Yoshi leaned back on the sofa and bit into a cream-cheese bagel. I chuckled as I studied the label on my apple-juice bottle. Robin wasn't convinced. "I don't know, Yoshi," she countered, picking hesitantly at a brownie. Short and round, Robin Stein was always on a diet. "It's probably some first-year schlemiel who's petrified. So every night he slips out in the hall and sets some toilet paper on fire to prove to himself he's not a wimp." Robin was a second-year whiz. She hadn't been invited to join the staff of Yoshi's journal but had successfully competed for a position on a less prestigious one. Like Yoshi, she already had an offer to work during the summer as an associate at one of the midtown firms. My thoughts wandered to the stack of polite rejection letters on my desk that could have all been addressed to "Dear Loser." "So, Janet, who do *you* think's doing it?" "Think? I *know* who it is. It's *me*!" They started laughing. "You are *such* a clown." "No, really, it is." Their laughter grew louder. The previous week, I had made the same confession to another friend; she didn't believe me, either. Their disbelief amused me. I suppose it was just too implausible. "And she manages to keep a straight face, too. That's what gets me," said Yoshi, laughing and shaking her head. I stood. "Well, I gotta go see a man about a horse." "See ya," called Yoshi. "Don't forget 'Death Warmed Over' this afternoon" —our name for Trusts and Estates class. "How could I, it's so fascinating!" I had actually planned to skip class because it conflicted with an important appointment I had, one with the law-school psychiatrist.

Within the university health service, the law school has its own psychiatrist, who works exclusively with law students. Something about the "unique nature of their pressures and stresses," according to the brochure. I had been seeing the suitably named Dr. Block, off and on, since my arrival. At my first appointment, I told him about the rape and my fear of the pent-up rage in me that seemed always on the verge of exploding. "Miss McDonald, you're going to end up either in prison or in a hospital." That was it. No concerned suggestions or helpful recommendations, just a casual death sentence. Unfortunately, he was all there was for law students. My anguish about the fires had reached an unendurable level. A shrink should understand and help me. I would confide in Dr. Block. I had no one else, really. My school chums didn't believe me, I had no close friends, and the only intimate relationship I was emotionally capable of was with myself, and that, only barely.

Washington Square Park stood between my dorm and his office. As I made my way, the cold February air held my breaths in smoky puffs. A gauntlet of drug dealers had replaced the guitar-strumming hippies who used to people the park; they whispered as I passed by, "Got that smoke, got that smoke." "What ya lookin' for, sis, what ya lookin' for?" I ignored them. Safely on the other side of the park, I pushed open the door to the health service. A bell jingled and the receptionist looked up over the top of her glasses. "Yes?" "I have an appointment with Dr. Block." "And you are?" "Janet McDonald." She examined her appointment book. There was a problem. "We do have you marked down, but he's not here." "He's not here? But I was supposed to see him at . . ." "Dr. Block is in a very important meeting with the dean. About those fires. Would you like to reschedule? He can see you in two weeks . . . Is Thursday the twelfth all right?" I was torn between laughing and screaming. "Yeah, that's fine." I didn't bother to write it down.

The Hayden Hall security guard, a friendly Haitian with whom I sometimes practiced French, nodded hello as I walked in. That Block, what a moron, I fumed, couldn't he at least have had the courtesy to cancel with me beforehand, rather than just blowing me off? A stereo was blasting Jim Morrison's "Light My Fire." Someone with a wry sense of humor and very loud speakers. In the dorm's game room I dropped quarters into the Asteroids video machine slot and began playing. The game demanded intense concentration, nimble dexterity, and tireless self-defense. I spent large amounts of money at Asteroids machines throughout Manhattan, fighting off onslaughts of tiny aggressors. The big, slow-moving asteroids were the easiest targets to blow apart. As they broke up, each piece picked up speed, until the dangerous small fragments were darting at me from every direction. The dean of students happened to walk by. I was embarrassed to be caught playing a teenager's game. Dean Rawls was the school's only black dean, hired as a result of pressure by black students on the administration to employ more people of color. He was easygoing and approachable. Maybe I could talk to him. "How ya doin?" he asked casually. "Good." I tried to feel him out. "So . . . what do you think about these fires?" He shrugged and said it wasn't any big deal, really, just some white kid acting out. "Yeah," I agreed. He wished me a nice day and I turned my attention back to the game. My shooter had already been blown to bits.

A few days after my encounter with Dean Rawls, the fire marshals came to Hayden Hall to conduct a room-to-room inquiry into the fires. It was exam season and the students were desperate to get the pyromaniac out of their lives. But not everyone welcomed the arrival of the marshals. I certainly didn't. It was rumored they were violating the students' Fourth Amendment rights and were targeting black men. One black student had broken down in tears during a lengthy grilling about a book of matches in his pocket. Apparently, he had told the marshals he was a nonsmoker, which, they said, was inconsistent with possession of a matchbook.

The marshals had made it to the fourteenth floor. Kim and I looked at each other when the knock sounded at the door. I answered, expecting to see rubber boots and shiny helmets. Instead, there were two guys in ordinary street clothes, one chubby and pink, probably Irish, the other lean and ruddy. Each of them had a noticeable bulge under his suit jacket. That, I didn't understand. Weren't fire marshals investigators who worked for the fire department? Why did these two have the menacing feel of cops? My temples throbbed. "Hi." I smiled. "As you know," the chubby one began, "we're investigating the fires in the dorm." To minimize our anxiety, the lean one assured us they were "interviewing" everybody, not just us. I relaxed a little. It all sounded rather informal. We were asked if we had "any ideas, any suspicions, anything." Obviously, *they* didn't. Kim said she didn't know anything. I said the same thing. Was there anyone, anyone at all, even the slightest doubt . . . No, we said, sorry. Yes, we would let them know right away if anything helpful came to mind. The entire interview lasted less than ten minutes. When they were gone I rushed downstairs to play Asteroids. When I returned, Kim was gone.

Willie and Florence McDonald in 1948. They had been "up North" for three years

I grew up in an old-fashioned American family headed by a traditional hardworking father and a tireless mother who stayed home to have children. Top row: Ann, Janet, Florence, and Willie. Bottom row: Ernest and Luke. Victor, Jean, and Kevin were not yet born

Daddy as Superman

A view from the projects

I had plenty of playmates when I was growing up in the projects. That's me on the bicycle

We knew all the soul hits by heart and formed singing groups that crooned "My Girl" or "Baby Love." Ann (far left) and two friends donned black sequins and became the Primettes

At fourteen, I already felt depressed and trapped

Bonding with Kevin during my first year of high school

With teenage fervor, I embraced every aspect of the times—I protested the war, marched for women's rights, and danced at Central Park "Be-Ins"

Daddy and Mother sending me off to Paris for my junior year abroad, 1975. In my fashion-don't polyester pantsuit and mustard-colored shoes, I certainly didn't look as if I was on my way to the world's fashion capital

While at Columbia Journalism School, I had my hair chemically straightened and styled like "Nancy Newscaster"

Hanging out with Denise (center) and another friend at a Paris café during my AFP internship

At thirty-two, years after my Cornell classmates, I graduated from law school. Here I celebrate with Kevin (wearing slip-on gold tooth) and Mother

For my NYU Law School graduation we rented a 1956 Rolls-Royce. The white, uniformed chauffeur seemed genuinely pleased to participate in the fantasy of a project family

At the law firm's country-club outing, I took golf lessons and smoked an awful cigar at dinner, hoping to bond with partners

Beaming in the City of Light. Photograph by G. Rae Wock

Playing Asteroids had made me more tense. I sat on my bed, leafing through the Corporations casebook. I was off the hook this time, but I knew things couldn't continue as they were. There was a knock at the door. I thought it might be Kim, having once again forgotten her key. I opened the door. It was the same two fire marshals. They just had a couple of follow-up questions. "Sure," I said, trying to sound casual. The darker one did the talking this time. He understood, he said, that law school was stressful, really hard on people, especially if you were new to a school and maybe had few friends. My breathing grew shallow. I wasn't getting enough air.

I was easy prey to their good cop–bad cop manipulations. The one warned, "Look, we can do this the hard way, or we can do it the easy way. Your roommate says she noticed that you leave the room and come back in before every fire, then the alarms go off.

You're setting these fires, aren't you, Janet?" The other condemned the "terrible, terrible thing that happened at Cornell that no one should have to go through," and wrapped his arm around my shoulders as I started crying. I had never been questioned by the police. I didn't know how to defend myself, and my loose grip on the situation faltered. Part of me said it didn't matter, that I would at last be able to extricate myself from the vortex that was swallowing me. Had I even been savvy enough to refuse to answer questions or demand a lawyer, I might not have done so. I was exhausted from my turmoil and acting out and just wanted it all to end.

I asked, my eyes on the floor, "Am I gonna get thrown out of school?" I'd recently celebrated Mother's birthday with her, and her joyous face now came to mind. "If you cooperate, we'll talk to the dean and do everything we can to help you. You'll probably just have to get some counseling." They said I had to go with them. "Listen, we won't even put the cuffs on you. We'll all just walk out like nothin' happened, and you can give us a statement downtown." They were so kind and sympathetic, my new cop friends. I reached for *The Phantom Tollbooth*, a children's book I'd been reading. "Can I bring this?" I needed to hold on to something familiar. They exchanged puzzled looks but said I could. It was past midnight when I walked out of Hayden Hall "like nothin' happened," an armed fire marshal on each side of me. Downstairs, my security-guard friend looked in consternation at the three of us, understood at once, and quickly looked down. For the first time, I was in the back seat of a police car as so many friends from home had been, just another project girl in custody.

At the precinct, I gave them the written statement they had requested in the dorm, and asked if I could leave. My new friends' attitude changed. I was abruptly informed that I was under arrest, and would be booked and arraigned with all the other "arrestees" picked up that night. "But I thought you said . . ." I protested weakly to the one who'd comforted me when I was crying. "Look," he snapped impatiently, "you already signed a statement. It's over." I felt light-headed. How could I have been so naïve, no, so outright stupid? These were cops making a bust, not compassionate friends out to help me. What a pathetic sight I must have been to these seasoned detectives, a young black woman under arrest clutching a children's fairy tale, asking if she could go home. Did I want to call my mom? they asked. "No." How could I possibly want to call Mother from a police station? She might drop dead. I thanked God Daddy wasn't around. I looked at the metal desks, the "Wanted" posters, and the big guns dangling from the hips of my jailers. Nothing made any sense and I felt helpless. The ruddy cop softened. "Listen, you should at least call your mom," he said, handing me the phone.

I couldn't. I took the phone and dialed Nikki Jones's number. She was married and living in Harlem in anticipation of the widely awaited Harlem renaissance. "Nikki, it's Janet." *"Salope!"* she exclaimed, using the French word for "bitch," our usual greeting. "What's up?" "Well . . . I've been arrested for arson and this is my one phone call and I'm too ashamed to call my mother," I blurted. *"What?!"* She was flabbergasted. I told her the story. "You *have* to call your mother, Janet." I promised to let her know what happened and hung up. The cop addressed me again. "Did you call your mother?" "No. I'm too ashamed." He said firmly, "You better call your mom," and offered me a second phone call. "Hi, Mother. Yeah, fine. Um, I just wanted to tell you . . ." I said there had been some fires in the dorm and the cops thought I had done it, and were questioning me at the precinct. "Oh, my Jesus! Don't worry, honey, they'll find who did it. If you didn't do it, you don't have a thing to worry about." That was precisely the problem. I said I was to be arraigned in criminal court in Manhattan the next morning, and she promised to be there. "Mother loves you."

I was distraught. Despite some sensational falls, I had remained the family's darling overachiever. My successes had compensated for my siblings' failures—the drugs, the arrests, the early pregnancies. Everyone had turned out bad except me, and I'd taken pride in my golden sheen. Now my mind veered from one ruined accomplishment to another.

"This way, ladies." Chained together at the waist, we "ladies" were being ushered toward the Department of Corrections van that would transport us from the police station to the Tombs, the holding pen of the Manhattan Criminal Court building. In that infamous spot we would remain in custody until the morning arraignments. Since I had been arrested late, I was in with the nighttime arrestees, a couple dozen tightly clothed, high-heeled prostitutes. I looked starkly out of place in my pea coat, jeans, and wire-rimmed glasses, clutching a book. "What'd they pick *you* up for?" exclaimed the driver as I climbed the three steps of the van. "Arson." His eyes opened wide. "You not the one who burnt up all those people in that hotel, are you?" It was my turn to exclaim. "No! That wasn't *me*." At least I could be proud of *something*. I took a seat and through the steel window grates watched the flicker of city lights as the van rumbled along on its nightly journey.

The intake officer was a black woman who appeared to be close to my age. I smiled and said "Hi," but her bored, indifferent expression didn't change. She said, "Surrender all personal items." After confiscating and inventorying my things, she gave me back my book, once she'd carefully flipped through the pages. I was led to a large, bench-lined cell with a bare toilet in the middle of the floor. I vowed to burst before subjecting myself to *that* humiliation. The "ladies" relaxed into a casual discussion about the big hotel arson. "I could see burning down shit for some money, like that arson-for-profit kinda thing, but doin' it for free, just to burn down shit, that's freak." "You got *that* right. You gotta be one *dumb* muthafucka to do it for free." They laughed. The teenager who'd been eyeing me curiously tapped my arm. I flinched. "Yo, so what you in for?" I wasn't about to admit to being a "dumb muthafucka." "Uh . . . fighting." "Ohhh"—she nodded—"you got into it in a club?" "Yeah," I said, like I brawled every night. "Don't be scared, they'll let you go. Ain't no thang. Hey, can I lay my head on your lap?" Scared to say no, I acquiesced. I didn't ask her why she was in custody. She might have killed the last person who refused to serve as her headrest. She lay down. I balanced my book on her shoulder and pretended to read, barely breathing.

A prostitute strolled over to the toilet. I kept my eyes on my book, the only anchor in my nightmarish journey. Another conversation got underway. A woman with a deep Brooklyn accent was saying, "Whaddya mean? There gots to be a Gawd, or there wouldn't be a woild. I mean, like, how you think we got here? Me, I don't care what you girls say—I believe in Gawd, and Heaven and Hell and the whole shebang." I couldn't believe my ears. A skeptic spoke. "Oh, honey, puh-leeze. That ain't nuthin' but fairy tales and you know it." The Brooklynite took umbrage. "Oh fuh Chrissakes, gimme a break, why don't cha? Widdat attitude, you'll be the first one dancin' on hot coals!" I hid my laugh inside a cough. "Nah, nah, hole up—you gon sit there and tell me Christianity is the only thing out there? That's out! They got the Buddha, Allah, them Hindus, them Jehovahs, it ain't just about Jesus." Someone summed up the irony of it all, and I could no longer keep myself from giggling. "Now, ain't *that* a bitch—a buncha hoes arguing about God! I dun heard just 'bout everything now!" I remembered religion class at Vassar, and thought how much more interesting my cellmates would have made it.

We were separated and placed in smaller, two-bunk cells. My new roommate stepped out of her three-inch heels, hopped up on the top bunk, and immediately fell asleep. I had grown up with bunk beds. I always got the queen-of-the-mountain top bed because Ann was too lazy to climb the ladder. The current arrangement painfully underscored my reversal of fortune. I crawled onto the lower bunk. Unable to sleep, I got up and just stood there. The light of early morning was beginning to rise. I looked at the cell bars, my book cover, the form of a sleeping prostitute. The trial came back to me. I saw the school class, the rapist's hateful stare, the bird. I had put the man behind bars with my testimony, and he had put me behind bars with his violence. We were both guilty, but he deserved prison, not me. After the rape I'd found no help anywhere—not at home, because I couldn't talk about it at all; not with friends, because I talked about it too much, and no shrink could cope with my anger and depression. Now this. I was suffocating and called into the empty corridor, "Excuse me! Officer? Officer!" No one came.

"Mc-Don-ald! Mc-Don-ald!" A stout black guard was calling my name. I leapt to my feet. *"Yes!"* "Come with me." My teeth were furry, my hair was in clumps, and I hadn't slept, but I was overjoyed—I had survived a night in the Tombs and was getting out! The guard led me into the open courtroom and motioned to a row of wooden chairs against a wall. "Take a seat until you're called." I sat next to the ladies of the previous night, now smeared and rumpled. Mother was seated in the front of the courtroom. Her tired smile and listless wave seemed to say, "Ain't no rest for the weary," one of her favorite maxims. Once again, it was proving true. I waved back, promising myself to make this up to her. Luke and his partner, handsome in a white navy uniform, were next to her, and Yoshi and Robin a few rows back. I was surprised to see them, having feared my schoolmates' reactions. I berated myself for the distress I'd caused everyone. The bailiff called my name and case number, the judge set a court date, and I was released on my own recognizance. I dashed through the waist-high swinging gate, into Mother's embrace. "I'm sorry. I feel like I let the family down." "Maybe the family let *you* down," she responded. Yoshi and Robin kissed and hugged me and told me not to worry. I went home.

Ernest followed me into my room, shaking his head in dismay. It was painfully obvious which of the two "graduates" had gotten the most from their education. "*Damn*, sis," he said, "don't you know you never say *nothin'* to no *po*-lice! I would've schooled you on that, but I never thought you'd be gettin' hooked up that way! Never say *nothin'* to no police. Everybody's hip to that!" I was embarrassed and made no response. He kissed me on the cheek and left.

By my deed, I had failed as a law student; by my confession, I had failed as a project girl. Ivy League peers and professors asked: Why? Why would a bright young law student choose to destroy her future? Vassar, NYU, a promising career . . . It just didn't make sense. It must have to do with the projects. Neighbors asked: How? How could a project girl who had grown up with some of the savviest criminals in the 'hood be so dumb as to cry on a lying cop's shoulder and confess to something no one could prove? Vassar. NYU. That's what it was, that naïve college-girl shit.

The phone didn't stop ringing for weeks. Most of the calls were from Vassar friends offering support. One former Vassar friend took a different approach to my misfortune, finding a way to turn it to her advantage. She gave the Vassar yearbook to her editor at a New York newspaper so my graduation photo could run with the story. Mother became hysterical when she opened the newspaper. "What are they trying to do to you?!" I was too numb to care. Did it really matter? Everyone knew anyway, thanks to the black dean. Dean Rawls's office had specifically named me in a flyer announcing the arrest and distributed it to the press and throughout the school. His move, approved at the highest levels of the administration, was sharply criticized by the black law-students association. In an open letter to the school newspaper, they condemned the measure as being "contrary to one of the most basic tenets" of the law—the presumption of innocence; arrest did not mean guilt. Disgust with Rawls was particularly acute because he had not revealed the name of a white student suspended for falsifying grades when his office publicized that incident. He hadn't wanted to hurt her career, he said. And mine? It was thought that, as the lone black dean, Rawls had jumped at the chance to prove he would not be inappropriately "black-friendly." I agreed, and was as hurt by the administration's reaction as I was moved by the students' compassion. Still, I had done it and was willing to face the consequences. In fact, I *wanted* my punishment. I hoped it might ease the pain.

Law students can be a notoriously career-oriented lot, interested in cultivating connections more than friends. And I had just short-circuited. It wasn't surprising, then, that many of them vanished. Maybe they had heard New York's "All news, all the time" radio station announce and reannounce my arrest every fifteen minutes. A former Vassar dean phoned when she heard it. "Each time they said your name, I couldn't believe it! Are you all right?" Of course I wasn't. Mother screened my calls, as I couldn't bear to talk to many of the callers. But at least one call was welcome. "Sweetie, it's for you. A Mrs. Younger from Cornell." I ran to the phone. I valued the support she gave me at Cornell and knew I could rely on her in any crisis. In her characteristically direct way, the first thing she said was, "Did you do it?" She was a tough lawyer and sounded prepared to defend me herself if I hadn't. I wanted so much to give her the answer I knew she hoped to hear but I couldn't. There was silence. She said that if I needed anything, anything at all, I should call.

Neighbors called with legal advice. "Yo, don't even bug about it. What they got you for, that ain't shit. The white man don't want *none* of us to make it, that's wassup with that. So check it out, when I got busted I found this straight-up lawyer. You pay only when the shit's over, and if you get time, you don't pay a dime. You got a pencil?" Others seemed almost relieved, as if I'd come home and was one of them again. Besides, run-ins with the law are not foreign to project people. Those who *haven't* been busted are the ones who stand out. Admittedly, my situation was a little different. School administrators had vowed in the newspapers to push for full prosecution, which could mean twenty-five big ones. Locking me up for a couple of decades would certainly placate angry students and alumni donors. The thought of a project college girl going to prison for twenty-five years who hadn't even killed anybody was staggering. A saying I had often heard in the neighborhood echoed inside my head, "Don't commit the crime if you can't do the time." My fifteen minutes of Warholian fame were not feeling very enjoyable at all. The student newspaper ran pro and con letters for months, arguing over what should be done with, or to, me. A prison inmate sent me a letter expressing his admiration for my "political action against the oppressor." A talk-show producer contacted my lawyer, asking if I would agree to be one of the guests on an arson panel. I was banned from campus, and school security guards were alerted to keep me out. Whenever I was in the neighborhood, I settled for a park bench in Washington Square Park. One day I was sitting there, sadly watching students go about their activities. A young Asian woman in jeans and sneakers approached. "Are you Janet McDonald?" I hesitated for a second before saying yes. She leaned forward and hugged me. "I'm a first-year and I just want you to know that I was with you when you were setting those fires!" All I could think to say was, "Oh! Uh . . . thank you."

Despite my "fans," an immense sense of shame shrouded my notoriety. I was in an ocean of despair and yearned to erase my strange new present and become a student again. I struggled to understand what had happened. I was indeed a strange hybrid of my disparate experience: a naïve Ivy League project girl whose potential for success seemed repeatedly to collide with an internal rage. There were court appearances and postponements, and finally, in light of the extenuating circumstances, I was given probation and a shrink's address.

More punishment came in quite an unexpected form. The rapist's appeal had failed, but now he had an even stronger weapon to use against me—me. The prosecutor on my arson case decided that those same "extenuating circumstances"—i.e., my past emotional turmoil—might have caused the rape jury to view me differently, had they been told about it. Since they hadn't been, he argued, the rapist didn't get a fair trial. A new trial was granted, but the Ithaca district attorney refused to retry the rape case, even though I begged him to do so. Consequently, the rapist had to be set free, after serving only three years of a twelve-year sentence. Appearing together on a television talk show, the ex-con grinned and talked about freedom, and the prosecutor touted his good deed. Later the lawyer, buoyed by the free publicity, left the prosecutor's office for private practice and the rapist returned to the streets. I would never be safe.

12

New York: February 1983–July 1984

In *Victims*, the woman played by the actress Kate Nelligan shoots her rapist dead. That was great, especially for television. The relationship between rapist and victim is struck through possession —he possesses you against your will. That possession continues until one of you dies. He is always *your* rapist: not *a* rapist, or *the* rapist, but *yours*. He belongs to you, as you belonged to him. And you are forever his victim until that relationship, created through violence, is severed with violence. It's not like a lover who becomes an ex, to be eventually forgotten. The rapist always exists in the present, my rapist, not my ex-rapist. We cannot negate his impact, or his ongoing power to haunt the mind, so we must kill him physically.

I have joined the Army National Guard. From Ivy League to green fatigue. Vassar goes military. I aced the Army Aptitude Test with a perfect score of 100, which thrilled me, and enlisted on December 1, 1982, swearing to something I was too amused to even hear, sticking my right hand defiantly in the air, close to laughter. It is interesting that army life, with all its discipline, rigor, structure, conformism, etc., would mean for me a gesture of "fuck you" to the world, a more sophisticated and complex way to act out. I signed up for the "small arms repair" unit, so I can learn how to use weapons to kill. I have not yet undertaken basic training, nor have I experienced actual army life other than a weekend drill per month. Thus, much of my idea about the military is based on fantasy—a combination of the fun and frivolity of the movie *Private Benjamin* and the muscled heroism of Yukio Mishima. Last month I had my very first drill at the Kingsbridge Armory. The impression I had of my future colleagues was: "Where did they get these people?" I was shocked. A stream of profanity coupled with a wealth of sexism and racism. Women are called "females," blacks call each other "niggers," and whites are "white boys." I also hear women referred to as "*that*," i.e., "I want some of *that*," or "*That* looks good." I felt disoriented, suddenly transported from the intellectual, feminist, racially ambiguous milieu in which I have nurtured myself. The positive aspect of all this is that the military offers a socially acceptable outlet for aggression and misanthropy, of which I have plenty.

I took the Officer Candidate School test about three weeks ago and learned just today that I passed, qualifying with a "90 or above." I begin officer training in June of 1984. How ironic I should find myself in the army in that ominous Orwellian year. I got the highest grade in my unit and the captain ordered me to his office so he "could look at the soldier" who scored higher than him! Acing the basic aptitude test is one thing—it wasn't very challenging. But scoring better than my own captain . . . wow! I was so proud, standing before him "at ease," saying, "Yes, sir, thank you, sir," knowing I beat a white military male at his own game. This is all so bizarre, though. Where is Janet who used to cry in bed about the Vietnam War, who tried to be politically correct—leftist, peacenik, Black Panther, environmentalist, anti-nuke and save-the-whatever? I believed in all that once and still do, in fact, except that now I believe without caring. Guru Maharaj Ji. Spirituality. Love. All gone. I have embraced Thanatos in myself, and therefore am drawn to manifestations of Thanatos in society.

I've been reading my SMART book (Soldier's Manual Army Testing) to prepare for basic training. I'm also learning how to dismantle, clean, and reassemble M-16 rifles.

I hope I can leave for basic by April and be back in New York in time to start Columbia Journalism School! Yes, I found out today that I have been accepted. I just happened to call to set up an interview, thinking, probably foolishly, that the "personal touch" might help my cause. The admissions person told me I had been accepted already and that they were "very impressed" by my application. What a rush! I am very happy. After NYU, I need every ego boost I can get. Is the best revenge the pen or the gun? I don't know.

Working as a paralegal in my new law-firm job. In the interview I used the excuse that I took off a year from law school to experience law practice firsthand. I just returned from drinks with Floyd Abrams (aka "Mr. First Amendment"), Sidney Zion of *The New York Times*, and some colleagues. What an exciting, interesting evening. First, we attended a New York County Bar Association–sponsored panel on the First Amendment. Zion is a colloquial wit who looks his age but seems about twenty in terms of hipness, demeanor, and perspective. He wears a gangster hat, has an angry street-kid attitude—i.e., "the whole system is corrupt"—and was on the David Letterman show last night. Abrams is wonderful—deeply intelligent, beautifully well-spoken, humble, and modest. A balding, affable, reasonable lawyer. I find him diplomatic and eloquent. They both came out strongly in favor of the First Amendment, freedom of the press, and allowing the press in courtrooms. It is interesting to be in the presence of the true power brokers of this country. Both Abrams and Zion have tremendous influence on the media, on the legislature, and consequently on my life. At first, I felt hostility toward the whole power-broker panel, then I began to feel excited, as though I, too, can be like them. I can share in their power and have impact on the world just as they do, even in opposition to them if I want.

It's so tempting to want the social successes of an Abrams or Zion, especially for a project girl like me. Shit, I am (was) a poor black child from a big, fucked-up family who was born and raised in a low-income housing project. I was smart, sweet, motivated—if I'd had fewer external negatives to struggle with and more of the protections and advantages that come with class, I might not have had the emotional warping I've had. But I was born in the wrong social milieu and that accident of birth has already hurt and thwarted my abilities and potential considerably.

A snowstorm has descended on New York City. It is awe-inspiring, numinous. The pelt of white powdery snow is accompanied by a fierce wind that whips it all about, sometimes blindingly, and a strange electric lightning that doesn't appear in the sky like a bent line but flashes broadly, lighting up everything for a startling second, the whole space around you. The wind was so strong I had to walk backwards all the way to the projects from the subway—it was a little frightening. Mostly, though, I was thrilled by the hush the snow brought to the city. It's as though the majesty of the storm is so overpowering that you feel you should speak softly out of respect, as though faced with something sacred. Yet there is confusion everywhere, deep in this silent white snow-blanket: stranded motorists, closed shops, scattered umbrellas. What we have, in fact, is natural anarchy, nihilistic nature. No business as usual these days; we're being compelled to think, be imaginative, ski to work. At work, Floyd Abrams called me on the phone to ask me to work with a new partner on the *New York Times* case. I was thrilled and honored. Is that jerky of me? I mean, this snow has stopped even Floyd Abrams's car.

I feel weird today. Thanatos on the rise. Anxiety. I called Dr. Gaines, who was rude and short with me. She promised to call back but didn't. I was at work until 9 p.m. but did nothing but laugh hysterically. Today is February 15, Ann's birthday. Thirty-two. She's so ravaged. Sad. Such absolute self-destructiveness. Me, I just want to kill other people. I'm writing lazily, too tired to plunge into my feelings and impulses, to analyze. I think it's only natural to be full of destructive rage against parents, family, institutions, the "law," shrinks, behavior and thought modification, adults, America. Will I be able to do my army push-ups and sit-ups tonight? The thought of basic training intimidates me. I'd rather keep working at the firm. Who needs discipline, structure, officer-candidate madness?

Attended another panel discussion on the First Amendment—this time its application to the judicial process, specifically in criminal cases. Again, there was Floyd Abrams, along with Mike Wallace and Roy Cohn. The fundamental issue was not addressed: the human impact, usually destructive, of publicity. I feel as though on one level my life has already been ruined by the publicity surrounding the rape and the fires. Life became sad in 1978 when Daddy died, but turned cruel in August 1979. I feel depressed, betrayed, ashamed, and most of all furious that I was raped and no one helped me, that I was overwhelmed at NYU and no one helped me, that I was wronged by the legal system and no one helped me. Not family, not friends, not any shrink, not a soul. And now Dean Redlich keeps me out of his school as if I am the criminal. It's no wonder that the only pleasure I get in trying to cope with all this is to fantasize about killing, annihilating the callous people who deliberately hurt or simply failed me.

My best buddy at work is Kenny Woo, a recent Columbia grad originally from Singapore. We laugh about how far from grace we have fallen, mere paralegals looked down upon by lawyers and secretaries alike. He got this idea that we needed to publicly confirm our genius by taking the test for MENSA, the international IQ society. Considering that neither of us has any self-esteem, it seemed like a good way to boost our egos. I took the test and passed! Kenny got in by submitting his Graduate Record Exam grades. He was afraid to actually sit for the test, which is mind-boggling: "If Mary has seven cousins and each cousin stands between 4'11 and 6'2, what is the circumference of the Earth on a rainy day?" Stuff like that. At least one thing to feel good about.

Vassar crowd birthday party for Adrian with the sons and daughters of wealth. No dancing, no drugs, no blacks besides me, but so what, no Japanese other than one painter. Conversation was pretty much null-and-void self-promoting chatter. I didn't talk much. Adrian, newly twenty-five, was in a Japanese getup made by one of the guests and seemed very tense and nervous. The day after, she told me she snorted a whole gram of coke by herself after the party was over.

Dead. Sick. I haven't written in weeks. Total relapse into self-hating, world-hating destructiveness. Dr. Gaines is shit, in a word. I've been on "vacation" for one and a half weeks. Some vacation—in the Farragut hellish wonderland. Reading *Women and Madness* (Chesler), which is lucid and enraging. Feel awful, useless, ugly, wasted, blocked. I have booked and unbooked trips to California, Virginia, and Hawaii, scheduled and canceled job interviews, purchased and returned circus tickets. Gaines is trying to dump me. Said I'm wasting my money and am stuck at a self-destructive place. She just needs the ego gratification of working with people who don't really need help, so she can feel like she's helped them. I fixed her, though—at the end of the session, at which she'd also complained about my hair (uncombed), behavior (childish), clothes (sloppy), and weight (skinny), I announced that I had no money for her (I had forgotten my checkbook). She got real pissed and authentic over *that*. No longer the distant, superior professional. "Janet, I want mah money!" It's hard though to break away from her emotionally. I admit to being a total jerk in therapy, but she responds jerkily, which is inappropriate for a shrink. My friend Gloria Brown says I am not having a useful relationship with Gaines and that she's "a waste." Gloria's right.

I want to go three or four times a week to the Metropolitan Community Mental Health Center. They are psychoanalytically oriented. Gaines says she does therapy, not analysis. Of course not—she's too much of a dolt to analyze anything.

Hell. Rock bottom and below. Crying in bed. Went to the Metropolitan Center. They wanted to commit me at St. Vincent's Hospital and threatened to call Mother about my suicidal/homicidal feelings and my gun. I saw a Dr. Wagner. He upset and scared me. Checked my bag for weapons. He said, "You have a lethal psychiatric disorder with a high mortality rate." Said my prognosis to live beyond five more years was in doubt. That I am probably smarter and have a higher IQ than my shrinks, which is bad for me because I play games and constantly show my shrinks how poor they are. He said, "You will keep winning at your games—you have to stop the behavior." We talked about my destructive urges. He was frightened by the affectless way I described holding an empty gun to my head, trying to imagine how blowing my brains out would feel. I said I had been raped and wanted to kill the man, now that he's out of prison. When I told him I carried a knife for protection (like the rest of New York), he made me put it on the desk, looked at it with horror, and said, "Jeez." He isn't sure the Center will take me. Back home, I went up to the roof and shot my gun at the sky. It was thrilling. A red flame leapt from the barrel. Loud. Must get a silencer. I felt powerful.

It's April and I'm already out of the army! Didn't survive the Officer Candidate School background check. I said the NYU fires were just firecrackers at a wild party but I was discharged anyway —the captain in Albany felt I was "hiding something." At least I got an honorable one. Still, it's humiliating. Once again, my fundamentally flawed self ruins opportunities my intellect creates for me. I'll never make it, never stop spiraling downward. How low can I go? Even the army—which takes anyone with legs and basic spelling ability—doesn't want me.

After I saw Dr. Wagner on Thursday I went a little crazy. The Center rejected me. Couldn't go to work Friday. Frantic and suicidal, I called Gaines everywhere, at all three phone numbers. Spoke to her domestic, Lilian. Fantasies of having her protect me from death and Thanatos. I just need her to help me but she isn't strong enough. I thwart therapy, yes, but a truly talented shrink should be able to deal with even that. I need help despite myself. She's good but I need a stronger hand. I think Dr. Wagner could help me but there's the potential for cultural distortions—he's a middle-class white man. I was in so much pain and really needed to talk to someone. Couldn't find Gaines, so I wandered around midtown and Grand Central Station, lost spiritually. She probably didn't return my calls because of the fuck-you letter I sent (800 fuck-yous). Plus, I'm behind in my payments.

I may need hospitalization. Wagner said I'd benefit from medication but he was afraid to give me any (suicide risk). If it can help I'll take it but I can't rule out a suicidal "gesture."

Ann tried to give me heroin yesterday. I was so devastated, desperate, and empty that I accepted it. But I gave it back—I don't want to be in cahoots with her.

I see why people become gun freaks. I hold an explosion in my hands, one that I can direct, like a thrown grenade, at anyone I wish. What power! The equalizer. My power was taken away from me by the man, my power to say no and have that respected, have my humanity acknowledged. When you say no and are ignored, humiliated, abused, and treated like a thing that has no opinion or wish worth listening to, then you are killed inside. The rape has killed me. I am dead.

Psychiatrists. Do you ever notice what liars they are? They steal glances at the clock, which is always at an angle where they can see it but I can't, and yawn through their noses, as if you're too neurotic to see their nostrils flare suddenly; they're bored but still pretending.

Everything I do unleashes my madwoman. It's like there's static electricity everywhere—soon you're afraid to touch any doorknob at all. I can't go out without the "kill drive" overcoming me. I want to blow my brains out in Dr. Gaines's lap or slip fifty lethal pills in my mouth while talking to her. I don't understand myself. I'm thirty years old and feel like a nothing because I don't accomplish anything in any realm. I don't accomplish anything because I don't try since I'm a defeated nothing. Then I'm depressed because I achieve nothing and therefore am nothing. Why can't I let my personal history fall away? Because it doesn't. It looks like my life will be like this until I die in five years, as per Dr. Wagner. If he was so worried and concerned as he claimed, why did he let the Center reject me? I'm going to call there and pretend I didn't hear from them, make them have to tell me why I was found "unsuitable." I'll just go underground and rob banks to survive. This Loeb needs a Leopold. The news said a Harvard Business School graduate killed her mom. I should write a book about Ivy League fury.

I am feeling human and hopeful and must write immediately, as who knows how long it will last. I got fellowship money to attend journalism school. I think I could be a good journalist if Thanatos would leave me. Spoke to three alums—it's exciting to meet intelligent black women who are nice. I never meet anyone intelligent, of any race.

The sadness of my solitude is immense. Others may glorify it, claim to "find themselves," thrive in their aloneness. If so, it must be of a different quality than mine, because the solitude I know devastates and empties the soul. These aren't merely words—it is literally true, and painful.

How does one *wake up* depressed? I have.

Lying in bed fantasizing about blowing my brains out, I heard Kevin say, "Salvatore's brother's dead." I jumped up. "Joe?" Yes. Joe is dead—he never woke up from his last drugged bliss. Sixteen years old. Poor Kevin. Joe was his friend and, unfortunately, role model (Joe had two guns, a safe full of money from various robberies, and a daring, reckless spirit. I admired him, too). I spoke to Joe a couple of weeks ago on the phone about needing another gun for protection. I promised to give him a hundred dollars for getting it, and he said, "Bet." Now he's dead. The same weekend he was supposed to get it for me, he was hospitalized for a cocaine overdose. Joe had a strong spirit. I bet he never lay in bed fantasizing about splattering out his brains. It's sad.

I certainly can't say I'm all right, because I know I'm not. Everything the shrinks say about me is true—revenge, acting-out behavior, rage, rejection complex, general inappropriateness, all of it. I probably do have a "severe chronic character disorder" if such a thing exists. The fact (and it is a fact that only two people really know) that I was actually raped seems of very little importance to anyone. Except me. The memory of testifying as he eyeballed me with his threatening gaze is still with me, weighing me down, wrenching my stomach, sickening me. He's from New York and could be here right now. Can I do nothing in the face of this abomination but hurt? That's what Dr. Gaines prescribes—swallow the pain, internalize the blame, victimize yourself. Me, I say fuck that.

Yesterday at work I bit the head off a rose on the twentieth floor reception desk to make the receptionist laugh. Floyd Abrams snubbed me earlier, by the way. Small matter.

I have a room of my own! I'm subletting Luke's studio on W. Seventeenth Street. I fall asleep with my hand on a gun, starting at small noises. It is strange living with myself. I am full of puzzling contradictions and complexities. Sometimes, I'm very emotionally ill and volatile, and other times strong, resilient, loving, and open.

Thanatos slipped up on me, I don't know exactly why. Tense inner silence, destructive impulses, remembrance of things past. I just got off the A train. The car was packed with thugs in gray-and-burgundy untied sneakers and color-coordinated jeans. They were hooting at women. Macho. Offensive by their very existence. If dogs run free (them), why can't we (women)? I wanted to machine gun them all, right there. I feel shaken with tension inside. Upon entering my building, I mistook a potted plant in the corridor for a man: my heart froze.

Mother told me a story about some project thugs fighting over a gold chain, one possibly losing an eye, and his teeth needing to be wired in. The deadly combination of ignorant materialism and psychotic machismo is what cost the boy his eye. It nauseated me and filled me with fear for Kevin at the same time that it reawakened my terror of street crime (and my hatred of thug punks). Gun and knife fantasies. When I came in tonight, I picked up my gun and searched the room for hidden assailants. I feel tight inside, unsmiling.

I dined at the Vassar Club. It was fun to be in such a preposterously plush place. The pianist played easy listening music and the food was delicious. Eli Wallach and Anne Jackson were sitting at a nearby table. I was with my friend Paulette, a feisty blond nurse from Brooklyn. Although Italian, she describes herself as "black-injected" because she had a lot of black friends in high school and dances well. She rankled at the sight of all the white-gloved black waiters in this posh Fifth Avenue club. "It's like a fucking slave plantation in here!" she said, and I agreed.

Sent off the following letter to the president of the New York Vassar Club: "I am writing to complain about the treatment I received recently at the Vassar Club. My attempt to enjoy a pleasant evening of conversation and dinner with a guest was marred by the insensitivity of the hostess and white waiters. Surely, it was just an innocent mistake that, upon seeing two women walk into the club, one black and one white, the hostess greeted the white one, the wrong one, with a cheerful, 'Miss McDonald?' And of course no harm was intended when our first waiter addressed my white guest as 'Miss McDonald.' And who would argue that our second waiter was anything other than a poor guesser when he handed the check to my guest, the white woman, the wrong woman. How ironic that my guest should be not only *not* the Vassar woman but not even a college graduate and that I should be the one with two graduate degrees. Whence, then, the presumption? Perhaps in her blond hair and blue eyes. The white one becomes automatically the right one. Some call it racism, the unconscious assumption that black means not as good, not qualified; in this case, not Vassar. Others may see it as an innocent mistake. Those others are in for a rude awakening."

Jean's boyfriend Wally was shot and killed two days ago. My nieces are going to the wake, which I don't like, but I may be wrong in my impulse to "shield" children from death. I was not touched, even though I used to see him a lot, hanging around Mother's, sleeping on the couch. I suppose I never cared for him that much—another slick, suede-shoed, street thug.

I'm listening to Albinoni's *Adagio*. Kevin left for the Job Corps Center in upstate New York, five hours away. Tonight is his first night "on his own," even though he is in a controlled, regimented environment. I bought him a newspaper, potato sticks, and Oreo cookies, having no money to give him. The other Job Corps people were very noticeable at Port Authority: black and Puerto Rican, all males. They were accompanied by hopeful and proud mothers and sisters waving goodbye as their little men were whisked away on Greyhound buses. Kevin cried—that is, he wiped a tear—smiling and waving. Mother cried at home. I was happy and relieved that he is no longer in the Ghetto Void, becoming null and void. The ball is in his court now.

Dr. Gaines harps about professionalism yet she fails to keep her personal feelings, attitudes, and values out of therapy. She creates stress instead of alleviating it. "Janet, get a haircut, why don't you wear makeup, you're prejudiced, you're an intellectual snob, but I can go one on one with you, you don't look clean, stop mooching off your mother, grow up and be responsible, you should make a contribution, you're not white so you can't kill people and plead insanity, you're paranoid—men aren't looking at you in the subway, if you're so funny why don't you do what Eddie Murphy does and make some money," etc., etc., ad nauseam. Curiously, her "blackness," on which she so solidly hangs her hat, has not enabled her to understand any more than other useless shrinks I've seen. She just wants me to be bourgeois like her and own an orange BMW and a Washington Heights brownstone.

My budding journalism career commenced with my missing the first day of school. Completely. Orientation, opening remarks, Circle Line boat ride, registration, everything. I didn't forget it. On the contrary, I'd spent plenty of *nuits blanches* awaiting the day with anxiety and sleepless nights, punctuated by nightmares. I just got my days and dates mixed up. Classes started Tuesday. Janet arrived Wednesday. Columbia is exciting, challenging, and stimulating; marvelously cerebral. I feel as if I've been stirred from stagnation, awakened out of a coma. This past week, I've been excited, scared, determined, intimidated, but not psychotic. I don't think acting out will be a problem. The students are congenial, impressive, diverse, international, and completely unlike law students; they know what camaraderie is. The teaching staff is funky and call themselves "editors," not professors. The first writing assignment I got was to interview a piece of "urban furniture." I went to the Village. My chosen interviewee ran away on skates, disappearing into an NYU building.

Floyd Abrams is my hero! He said yes, I could use his name as a reference. Yayy! He said also that he looked for me on the journalism-school boat ride. *Merde*. I'm taking law courses as part of my plan to enroll at Columbia Law School (fat chance) if NYU doesn't take me back.

I'm ecstatic! Chased a potential rapist off campus. There's a man, black or Hispanic I can't tell which, who loiters daily in front of the steps of Low Library, stealing looks under skirts and dresses. He ran off when I walked over to a young woman he was eyeing and told her what he was doing. I protected someone else as I wish I'd been able to protect myself. I wrote to NYU requesting readmission for next year. I have to go back and graduate or I'll hate myself for the rest of my life and feel like a loser. Unlike the rape, this is a trauma I can undo. The deal with NYU is that I must first be inspected and approved by a psychiatrist of their choosing—and they've chosen a Dr. Cancro of the NYU Medical Center. I already have an appointment. We'll see what happens. I signed up for two law classes. I can't fail in any of these endeavors, no matter how intimidating, arduous, or time-consuming. And I must keep my mental health. Columbia has great facilities.

Nightmares since school started. Usually of menacing men. But last night was a first—rats. Yes, there were about ten rats in here, coming out of a hole in the wall. The worst part was that I couldn't make them run away, which is the decent rodent thing to do. They just sat around calmly all over the place, as I grew hysterical.

Dejected about J-School. I don't write well journalistically, a teacher wants to "talk," I have no newsworthy ideas or savvy, and there's too much work. Law school is intimidating and I have a lot of reading. It's too clinical and I forgot how to do research. Can I make it this year? There is so much to achieve and no room for failure or flubbing. TV reporting is great. I love being on-camera, behind the camera, and in the editing room. The gentle enthusiasm of Professor Schultz is infectious. I like my group, too. But I'm bummed.

My emotional state has not been good. A week ago I met with Dr. Cancro, a solid, Italian-looking man who wears his hair combed straight back. I went in determined to fool him into giving me his seal of approval, but quickly gave up—he's too smart. I felt humble and helpless. His intelligence and non-maudlin sympathy made me like and trust him. I told him how afraid I felt that the rapist was loose again, how humiliating his early release was for me. Cancro didn't insult me by pretending I was safe, nor did he enrage me with accusations of paranoia or accolades about my victorious survival. He said the rapist is a psychopath and hates me because I sent him back to prison. I have no choice but to find the strength to cope with that reality. He brought up the unsuc-cessful coping strategies I have used in the past, like the fires. That was when the interview seemed to take an unfavorable turn. I had no reassuring sound bites, no facile explanations, no convincing guarantees. At the end, I asked if he intended to recommend read-mission. He was noncommittal. Luckily Bert, my new therapist at the university health services, is great. She called me several times this past week as I tottered on the verge of violence, despair, and suicidal feelings. Forget borderline, I've crossed the border and am on 40 mgs a day of Mellaril. Can't tell what it's doing. I told her I was fighting the medication, struggling desperately to preserve my identity, unaltered by psychoactive drugs. Delighted to have dumped Gaines, though.

Kevin was kicked out of the Job Corps for engaging in rowdy behavior with a bunch of boys. The whole family is cursed. We're the black, penniless Kennedys.

I have a perm! Yep. Janet McDonald has chemically straightened hair styled like "Nancy Newscaster." I don't care anymore—hair is no longer a political statement for me. Goodbye fourteen-year-old Afro, hello Sue Simmons.

Midnight. I imagined hearing a mouse, which generalized into hearing threatening sounds everywhere and getting out my gun, which I placed near the bed. Wrote Bert a crazy, rambling, childish letter full of despair, fear, and false bravado. She's very intelligent and astute. Calls herself "Mrs. Bertocci."

Another miserable night. Good conversations with Bert, who is trying to help me and "keep things to a dull roar," as she put it, through Mellaril and Asendin, both of which I stopped taking yesterday (they made me too glazed). I love her and promised to leave her my cat in my will.

School was harrowing yesterday. I was the on-camera reporter and froze when it was time to write my script under pressure. Our adjunct professor, Randall Pinkston from CBS News, was a godsend and quietly talked me through writing out the story very simply, one element at a time.

The world around me has a slightly changed aspect. Nightmarish faces, frightening and distorted. Instead of just walking down the street, I have the sensation of being in a long, deep canyon, concrete walling the sides, trapped as if in a maze. I feel danger inside me and danger all around, either very powerful and strong, ready to pummel anyone who bumps into me . . . or terrified. It feels like I've no control. I have been in and out of hell. Stood at a bulletin board with a matchbook in hand but stopped myself. Please God help me get through this.

I dropped State and Local Government. Too deadening. My hair is done in a newscaster perm which seems to make people, especially my family, respond to me more favorably. How annoying it all is. I must admit, it does look good, but it's not me. What is *me* anyway? Nothing. I've been choked up all day, heavy and tearful with depression.

I got a letter from NYU. It said Dr. Cancro had recommended I be readmitted. I cried. I'm not saying anything to Mother until I'm actually accepted, so I don't get her hopes up. There's still the school-interview hurdle.

NYU readmission interview. Six people around a conference-room table questioning me about the fires. Why did you set the fires? Why did you stop seeing Dr. Gaines? What precautions will you take? Why do you want to come back to NYU? Dean Redlich was seated next to me. "We want to protect you. We want open channels." Joyce Curll, the admissions officer who let me in in the first place, looked genuinely sympathetic. Dean Rawls was there, too, the traitor, and three professors. Very strange. Stressful. Me in pinstripes, mascara, straight hair. "I feel I owe a debt to NYU," I said, feeling more hostility than gratitude. It was like facing the Inquisition, and I loathed the feeling of being judged once again. Judges in courtrooms, judges in schools, judges in hospitals. But I was desperate for their blessing. The rape had driven me from law school, and now the two were inextricable. For my own sanity I had to get back in. If not, I would forever have to live with the knowledge that *he* stopped me from becoming a lawyer. My indifference toward the career gave way to zeal—I would become a lawyer, whether I really wanted to or not. "I want to practice law in the context of a news organization," I said. Later on, I had trouble locating my emotions—elation, depression, anger, numbness. Called Bertocci the next day. She is incredibly supportive of me. She is the only therapist who has given me the emotional help I've needed during therapy, the only one to really understand me, to seem to care.

It's a miracle! I'm going back to NYU law school! I go back next September. I did it! This will be my third time starting or restarting law school. They say three strikes and you're out. No more outs for me. I want to be perfect, make up for the fires. My whole being is a trembling thing, shaking with happiness. The acceptance letter came today. Mother had tears in her eyes reading it. "Oh, my Jesus." She kissed my cheek. I am golden again. The bad news is, I will have to see Dr. Block every week. Ugh! He's an obtuse, unhelpful dolt.

Someone in the family stole $250 from Mother and she was crying for days. I gave her $200 yesterday.

2:05 a.m. Two Secret Service agents picked me up tonight at the apartment: charge—making threats on the life of Gary Hart! I had come home from watching the Low Library presidential debate on television with Randy Johnson, a school friend. The agents had apparently been waiting for me in a car under the snowy, wet sky. I didn't see them. As I was unlocking my door, I noticed two strange-acting white men at the outer door. I wondered for a second if they were rapists. They flashed badges, asking, "Are you Janet McDonald?" Yes. Why? Inside, they patted me down. I repeatedly asked what this was all about, but they just kept saying, "We're Secret Service agents. We protect Presidential candidates. And you don't know what this is about?" I said I had absolutely no idea.

"Where are you coming from? What were you doing?" I told them I was at a friend's apartment watching the debate. Nightmare feelings of the fire marshals at NYU returned. I was shaking inside but tried to stay cool on the outside. "Keep your hands to your sides," they warned, and asked about guns or other weapons in the apartment. They wanted to search (I said no) and asked to use the phone (I said yes). "The suspect is in custody," the blond said into the receiver while the other one cuffed me ("This is for your own safety and our agents' security"). They were concerned that I might slip out of the cuffs because my wrists were so thin, so one held me by my arm at all times.

They put me in the back seat of a car and drove me down to the World Trade Center. People stared as I passed by in handcuffs, wearing a Columbia University sweatshirt. My heart was racing. They took Polaroid mug shots. "Smile," someone said. Someone had emptied the contents of my knapsack onto a table—credit card, Vassar Club and MENSA cards, a school paper, Cheez Doodles, a novel, and my glasses. I was taken to another room, where, to my horror, a woman agent told me to strip and bend over. I protested in vain.

Four agents interrogated me; others peeped in occasionally. Questions: What do you think of Gary Hart? What do you think of Mondale? Jackson? Have you ever hurt anyone? Do you own a gun, any weapons? Ever shot a gun? How long have you had emotional problems? One asked, "When is the last time you had a fight?" I said, "That's like asking, 'When did you stop beating your wife?'" He sneered. I said again and again that I actually liked Gary Hart and thought he was cute, all ears and cowboy boots, and had planned to vote for him. No one seemed to believe me. They wanted to know if I belonged to any organizations, and I mentioned MENSA.

My insides were cramping. Two hours later one of my interrogators said someone would drive me home. At the elevator, an agent said, "There's a fifty-fifty chance you've been set up. Half of us believe you and half don't. Don't take this personally. I wouldn't lose any sleep over it. People are assholes. I been in this business nine years and it makes you lose faith in humanity." He said they are obligated to investigate each and every allegation because the one time they don't, it could be the one time there's a real problem. I started thinking about obnoxious people *I* could accuse.

I was stupefied. Who would have done that to me? A jealous student? A teacher? All I could come up with was earlier that day I had covered Hart's campaign stop at Grand Central Terminal with my broadcasting-class crew. Maybe someone on campus, a hypervigilant undercover agent or something, overheard me talking about going downtown to "shoot" Gary Hart, and the person didn't know I meant with a camera. As I was leaving the car, the agent, named Farley, told me he'd spoken to Bert and Mother. Then he apologized.

I called Bert right away. She'd refused to tell them anything and kept gasping as I recounted the story of the handcuffs, strip search, questioning, et cetera. Farley hadn't told me that, before they picked me up, two other agents had gone to Mother's place and harassed her with talk about how I might get shot, to make her tell them who my friends are (as if she even knows). He also didn't mention that they questioned my seven- and eight-year-old nieces. I feel dull trauma. Did this really happen?

Agent Farley wants to pick me up again to take me downtown for a polygraph test. I panicked and called Paulette. She picked me up in her car and whisked me back to Brooklyn, cursing "those fucking assholes" all the way. I called the school; the news had already spread. Dean Johnston said the J-School had "cooperated reluctantly" and given my address to the SS. He also said now they were going to write a letter of complaint to the SS and ask that any files on me be destroyed. Yeah, right. I'm sure Agent Farley would agree to that right away. Columbia gave them my address! Idiots.

I'm scared. Agent Farley left a message on my answering machine threatening to "come on campus and ask questions" if I didn't come in for the polygraph.

Bert spoke to a high-level school administrator, she said. He promised to phone the SS and tell them to "call off their dogs."

I've been through the mill. I was at SS headquarters on Sunday from 10 a.m. to 6 p.m. My best friend from school, Karyn Korieth, stayed with me until about three—on her birthday! An agent named Maguire said when we first arrived, "Let me just talk to Janet alone for five minutes." That took until noon. "What did you say about Hart? Why did you set the fires? Were you on drugs or alcohol? Do you have memory lapses? Why did you leave Cornell?" ("I don't want to talk about that," I answered, knowing he was hinting at the rape.) Were you ever institutionalized? (I assumed they already knew about my stay at the state hospital in Ithaca, so I said, "That was only three days"; maybe they didn't already know.) I kept thinking, if I get through this I can stop this thing from spiraling, stop them from going up to Columbia asking others what *they* thought about the fires, the state hospital, etc. "Look, I want to get this thing over with as much as you do. I have more important things to do. It's the people in Washington . . ."

"Take the polygraph and that'll end it," they said. It was scheduled for one o'clock, but Agent Buckner didn't arrive until 2:15. She explained the machine to me. "The polygraph measures truth. It's simple. It measures the responses of your autonomic nervous system, which you can't control, and if you're not telling the truth it will show up, and if you are, that will show up, too. You look like an honest person; you wouldn't lie, right? I believe you're trustworthy and truthful and this machine will show it. You're going to answer all the questions truthfully, right?" She asked about memberships in organizations. I told her I was a member of MENSA and the Vassar Club. "What do they do?" "Nothing," I answered.

I was directed to a chair facing the wall. Right arm: a blood-pressure patch. Chest: a black coiled cord. Solar plexus: similar black coiled cord. Left hand: metal clips on two fingers. I was told to sit very still and not move. Buckner had me do a ludicrous exercise where I was supposed to lie about the number I wrote down on a piece of paper and have my autonomic nervous system squeal on me. "See!" she raved. "You're just like everybody else.

The machine showed you were not telling the truth." Then the real test began.

Is your first name Janet?

Is your last name McDonald?

Were you born in Brooklyn?

Do you intend to answer the questions about Gary Hart truthfully?

Did you say you want to shoot Gary Hart?

Did you ever betray the trust of someone who had confidence in you before your twenty-ninth birthday?

Did you ever lie to a person in authority before 1984?

I answered the questions three times. At 5 p.m. I was fed up with these lunatics and said I was going home. "I can't believe you don't want to clear your name! I came all the way down here, wasting my time!" "Well, I don't even want to be here. Anyway, I'm not wasting your time, your employer is." "This is my day off," she snapped. I persisted. "You said I could stop any time I wanted to." "That's right, go ahead. I can't believe after four hours you can't spend two minutes to clear your name." Agent Maguire rushed in. "What are you doing?" I said, "Look, the whole thing is ridiculous and I don't see how it depends on that machine. If you're not going to believe me, you're not. I never threatened Gary Hart." He said the polygraph would settle it once and for all if I gave them "just two more minutes." I acquiesced. After fifteen minutes of "analysis," Buckner announced, "The results are inconclusive." I wanted to laugh, and in fact smiled. She continued, "Look, we want to help you if you have a problem . . ." I just sat there looking at her. She started packing up the Truth Machine. "Can I go?" "Yes," said agent Maguire. "Thanks for coming down." Buckner was pissed and didn't say goodbye. As I was leaving, I overheard her saying to Maguire, "Very unusual." End of Sunday with the SS. Back home, my phone-machine message light was flashing. Bertocci had been calling me since 4 p.m. She was appalled by my story. Next I spoke to Paulette. "Why did you take the polygraph? Why didn't you tell them to fuck off?!"

Monday, I saw Bert; she was meeting that afternoon with agent Farley and Vic Daniels, the university's attorney. We parted and I went downtown to the Woolworth Building to see some private attorneys the university had recommended for a possible civil suit. The lawyers were outraged. Then came their questions. "Have you ever been arrested? Is there anything in your past that could hurt your case? Why did you leave Cornell?" I lied in response to all three questions, each one a little more painful. They said they'd call Farley the next morning. I knew the shit would hit the fan then. Farley would tell my real story, the lawyers would inform Columbia, and everyone would know about my lies and shame.

I was in a state of anguish and turmoil when I got home. I started calling Bert, Paulette, and Karyn . . . Couldn't get anyone. Six o'clock, seven o'clock. I took six Mellaril with beer, then some more, then more. I dialed Bert again and she answered, happy. "It's over," she announced, "and I was very pleased with how Columbia handled it." After the university's attorney warned the agents to leave me alone or face a lawsuit, the dogs beat a hasty retreat. "I'm very depressed. I don't want to keep living. Why won't you let me go, you know I'm miserable, that I'm suffering. The Secret Service thing was symbolic. Bad things keep happening to me. I'll never be happy. I don't want to struggle anymore. I left you my journal in my will." She asked me for Karyn's phone number but I wouldn't give it to her. "I don't want to be saved this time. I don't want to try." She assured me I was going to feel better. "No, I'm not. You're my therapist, of course, you think that." "You just need more treatment, Janet. Either I call Karyn or I'm going to have to call an ambulance. What have you taken?" I told her. "Can you give me your address? I don't want to get it from someone else, but I can. Please give me your address." I gave her Karyn's phone number and my address. The medicine and beer were affecting me. All evening I'd been listening to the sad songs of Léo Ferré, Jacques Brel, and Barbra Streisand. I had left notes with instructions as to what should be done with my belongings. All I wanted was to feel better, to stop hurting. Bert was saying that she wanted to get me to a safe place to spend the night, when I heard a knock at the door. "Janet, please let them in." Standing outside were two Hispanic policemen and two white EMS guys from St. Vincent's Hospital. "We were called about a drug overdose?" I made myself bright and chipper. "No drug overdose here!" They started walking away, calling in an apartment-number check on a walkie-talkie. I didn't want them to leave. "Here, someone wants to talk to you," I said, handing the cop the phone. Bert explained the situation and I went with them to the ambulance parked out front.

At the hospital I said, "Oh, nothing's wrong with me. Sometimes therapists overreact." The last thing I needed was another stigma attached to my name—a night in St. Vincent's psych ward. The admitting nurse was annoyed. "Well, I'm going to call her and find out who's lying! This is ridiculous." She headed for a phone to call Bert and I hurried out of the hospital and went home.

I lay in bed, panting. Every time I stood, I'd fall to the floor. I felt groggy and scared. I got Bert on the phone again. "I'm sick." She had Karyn come over. Karyn choked up when she saw the notes I had left, and didn't raise her eyes for a while.

Nightmare. Four Puerto Rican guys start pulling me somewhere, sex clearly on the agenda. I said, "Come on, guys. Don't hurt me, please." I was resisting, but weakly, and was skimpily dressed. I scream, but the sound is weak and ineffective. The guy drags me into the room, holding a broken piece of brown glass to my neck, yelling, "Why did you scream?!" His torso is covered with white paste and he's sweaty. I yell, "I didn't!" I awoke petrified.

I've managed to get back in the saddle, as they say. I choked down all the pain brought on by the Secret Service incident and am functional again. The Freedom of Information Act request I filed got me only a few pages of blacked-out documents. I guess I'll never know why they came after me.

Today was my AFP (Agence France-Presse) interview with a bald Frenchman who didn't succeed at putting me at ease. A mercifully short talk in French. He interviewed eight women and two men, of whom eight were American and two European. One black person. Me. I think that because the internship is for Paris they want someone white. Lee Edwards, the head of interns at *Newsweek*, called. "I'm so thrilled, I hope I'll make your day." She offered me a summer internship. I tried to sound effusively grateful but felt rather dry about it. It's just that I don't know what I want to do —print or broadcast, law school or not, summer job or permanent job or whatever. I only want to hoard weapons and kill rapists. And I don't want to leave "the fold"—school, Bert, or the other students, especially not Randy and Karyn.

Tears work wonders on contact lenses. I just returned from nine hours at home in the projects! It was hell. I couldn't look directly at Mother. She's heavy and has dark circles around her eyes. She looks resigned and miserable. It felt like everybody was clawing at me, tearing off a piece. I feel so bad for them and give what I have, but it's never enough. Kevin wants money and gold chains but only really acknowledges me in the house. Outside, I think he's ashamed because I don't dress hip by project standards (my jeans are unironed and lack sharp creases). My nieces want me to put them through dance school and take them to movies. Ann wants me to find her a job or an apartment. I've been crying. I want to go to Paris, change my name, and never return.

The guy from AFP picked me! The only bona-fide French major. My language skills were better than the others', who'd learned French by living there but didn't know grammar. Amazing, the steep ups and downs I'm having. Now I have two consecutive internships for the summer, first *Newsweek*, then AFP in Paris! And to think I was almost a suicide. The best revenge *is* success.

Well, I graduated. I arrived at Columbia in a silver stretch limousine with Mother, Paulette, and three nieces (out of four; Ann and Jean tried to come with the youngest, but they couldn't find Columbia. Duh!). Anyway, fuck Columbia! I'm pissed off. I was disappointed because I graduated without honors or prizes. I felt like a failure, a nothing, like my family wasn't proud of me. Dan Jones was number one in the class, not me. I should have been up there with a $4,000 Pulitzer traveling-fellowship check in hand, crying and mouthing maudlin thank-yous to significant people. Nobody black won anything. Lots of whites didn't get anything either, though. Mother said Daddy would have been proud. But why couldn't I have won some kind of award, anything? Paulette made me feel worse by asking, "Why didn't you get a prize? I wanted you to win something so badly. You're good." I felt I had let everyone down. I wasn't cheered when my name was called, like the students who carried their babies onstage. *Merde*. I was sad.

Newsweek. Yesterday I hated it but today I liked it. Nothing bad happened yesterday, I just felt weird, let down, forced into my Super Black-Whitegirl Vassar persona. I'm back in pinstripes, suits, and little black sensible shoes in midtown. Shit.

Newsweek sent me to cover Nancy Reagan at the Waldorf. I saw one of the Secret Asshole Agents who interrogated me at SS head-quarters. Security was so lax I walked right in with no ID check. Boring event. Ruffled sleeveless dresses, tuxedos, millionaires all over the place, Oscar de la Renta, William F. Buckley. The further I go in journalism, the greater access I gain to my enemies. At work, I act wide-eyed, eager, and polite, bending and scraping, laughing at everyone's jokes, brown-nosing. I hate this servility and feel like a Dostoevsky character: the sub-assistant to the assistant to the undersecretary's undersecretary. Like Golyadkin in *The Dou-ble*. My heart isn't into the corporate scene anymore. I can't play successful white male patriarch and power broker; it's bullshit, deg-radation, humiliation, and boredom. I won't "succeed." I won't be a journalist. I won't become like Lee, who has a completely anal personality; pure Vassar, right down to her Vassar College ring. Everything about her is long, angular, and pointed. She is six feet tall, skinny as me, and speaks with perfect articulation; she has precisely manicured flattop fingernails, impeccable clothes. "One should verify every sentence, every paragraph, even each individ-ual word!" she told me during my interview, clenching her fist delicately. "But one should never rely on a phone book." I wonder if she is demented; I feel weird in her presence. I saw Osborn Elliott on Madison Avenue today. To show off in front of Elsie Wash-ington, another researcher, I ran up to him, shook his hand, and said something inane and frothy about *Newsweek*. "Hello, Janet," he said, completing my victory by knowing my name. Elsie was impressed. Had I been alone, I would have ignored him. I'm sui-cidal, an overeducated slave on the bottom of the white patriarch's totem pole.

Elsie, who is black, told me, over lunch, "the real deal" at *News-week*. She said white males have everything sewn up. "A lot of these black kids think because they went to schools like Harvard,

Yale, Princeton, and Vassar that they've got it made. But once you're out here, you're just another black." Thanks for the pep talk. I can't make it in the rat race because I'm not a rat. I hate *Newsweek*.

I like *Newsweek*. The work is challenging and sometimes substantive, as when I reported and wrote the file on Nancy Reagan which everyone who commented (two people) seemed to like, although they didn't run the story (too uninteresting). I'm happy.

I went to work and had a good time, although I got a headache when I found in the clippings library three articles about me in the NYU file.

It's 10 p.m. If I'm never heard from again, that means the rapist got me on my way to the corner grocery store.

I made it back alive this time. Everyone is out in the warm night air enjoying themselves and I'm in here cleaning my gun, worrying about the rapist's whereabouts.

Newsweek is a morass of incest, nepotism, elitism, racism, and utter classic white male patriarchal corruption. Everybody is some robber baron's son, daughter, wife, cousin, or something, and they are the only ones to progress, meteor-like, from the researcher doldrums and into the ranks of writer, correspondent, and beyond. It is truly nauseating. Of course, one or two whitewashed black tokens move up also, but only to a certain level, before they hit the invisible race ceiling. It is completely Ivy League—a Vassar/Columbia J-School dumping ground. I benefited from that aspect of their snobbery but still detest it wholeheartedly. I went to the same schools as these people and shared, I naïvely thought, their world, but I will always be excluded, regardless of how many Ivy League degrees I acquire, because of the next level of hurdles: family connections and money.

I saw an interesting program about JFK on Channel 13. Born rich, there was nothing left for him to pursue except power. We poor lust for money and the freedom it affords. The rich, like JFK and ilk, worry about who is a blueblood and whose ancestors were "Irish potato pickers." JFK, a millionaire at twenty-one, and most certainly not self-made. Power, and the wrangling over it, is fascinating. As for me, I'm a void, grasping at superficialities like money, status, prestige, and glamour, but basically empty and idle. I don't know what I am or what I want to be.

Mother said Ernest got off on a gun charge and Ann is still running the streets. We're all going to hell, just like Daddy said.

This evening I was anxious and a little borderline, couldn't decide what to have for dinner, couldn't feel my emotions. Walked around midtown, down Madison Avenue, up Fifth Avenue between Forty-sixth and Fifty-ninth. Sat near the Plaza Hotel and looked at the wide pale sky over Central Park. Watched tourists pass by. I felt deep sadness and angst about living. Mixed in with that sorrow was a growing anger that developed into a dull desire to kill someone. When I got to Fifty-ninth and Lexington I started looking at the half-moon in the night sky and began crying for Bert. I can't believe I won't be able to keep her as my therapist. (I'm not enrolled at Columbia anymore and she doesn't have a private practice.) So there I was, crying in midtown, not wanting to live, wanting to destroy something. It hurt. I stopped eventually and went back to *Newsweek*. I realize I haven't been feeling my emotions lately because they're too painful. It's fucking not fair and makes me very angry and pissed. In the book *A Secret Symmetry*, the author refers to the therapist as the "treasure beyond one's grasp." That's Bert. I'll miss her very deeply. She's leaving a gaping silence in me where our voices used to meet, where I felt I was making a real human connection. I could die from the hole she's left in me. But she doesn't need me— her life goes on. There are no silences, holes, or wounds left in her, only the anxious, eager faces of the next batch of insane Columbia students waiting in the reception room to follow her down the corridor to her office. I hate her.

History is being made! Mondale has named a woman as his running mate. We may have a woman Vice President! I am very pleased, as she is a feminist and a liberal. Of course, the media are making a sentimental maudlin mush of it. This Ferraro choice is going to cause an uproar in the electorate. Some men just can't handle it. They feel their penises shrinking.

I'm free! My last day at *Newsweek*. Elsie gave me a sushi T-shirt. I must be excited about returning to Paris because I keep screaming in the subway as trains go by. I'm going to have a new life, brand-new. And Paris is such a feminine city—elegant, clean, refined, civilized. New York is so urban-intense. Goodbye little thugs in untied sneakers, serial murderers, nerdy law students, screeching train wheels, tacky news programs! I'm never coming back to this nightmare of terror, fingerprinting, mug shots, court appearances, bad shrinks, rape crisis, armed survival, misery, anomie, false friends, true enemies, medication, despair, draining family members, rape and rapists!

I'm on the phone with Lisa. She told me that police cars are all around her house: a woman was just raped in Riverside Park. Why did she have to tell me that? My guts convulsed and now I'm depressed. My whole mood has changed to one of sickness. I wish I could kill one before I leave—but if I do come back, that is going to be at the top of my agenda: an all-out war on rapists.

Paris: July 1984–September 1984

I've been in Paris a couple of days now (slept through one of them). I'm staying with my friend Puce, a Guadeloupian dancer, in the primarily North African twentieth arrondissement. She has a small studio with no refrigerator. It's nearly midnight and Puce and her African boyfriend just left to go sit in his car or something. Yesterday, I keeled over at 5 p.m. and awoke at 11 p.m., eager to start my day. Unfortunately, neither Puce nor the sun was ready.

I dreamed Geraldine Ferraro and I were discussing her candidacy for Vice President and I told her how important it was symbolically for women. She agreed. Two unshaven white men in their thirties appear. They are rapists. She looks at one of them in amazement and says, "You're going to do it again, aren't you?" He smirks and I wake up, knowing they raped her.

I had a pleasant day. A deep-blue sky, sun glistening on statues and fountains and leaves and windowpanes. I took the métro to the Tuileries and headed for Jeu de Paume. Instead of going there, I decided to sit on a bench, near the Maillol sculptures. Some guys who looked very American were playing Frisbee and one of them invited me to join in, which I was eager to do. We played for about a half hour before a park security guard put an end to the game. Our group consisted of two Danes, one Canadian, one Englishman, another American woman, and a woman from Peru (or Beirut, I'm not sure which she said). We talked some and then they went off to a bar to drink wine and beer. I slipped away, fearful of, I don't know, being bored, being ignored, getting drunk, maybe getting hurt. They were in Paris for only a few days, so it's not like I missed out on friendship. I lay down on the grass and lost myself in the magnificent sky, as in John Lennon's film *Apotheosis*. Later, I strolled down to the Place de la Concorde, where some women were modeling. One was very tall and blond, and strutted back and forth, prancing like a horse. She would stop suddenly and throw her hair across her face. At one point, an assistant went up to her and removed her bra, I guess to add some erotica. She was wearing high heels, black ski pants, a striped sweater around her hips, a white top, and a black jacket. All said, she was very *dramatique.* As another assistant was brushing her hair, she stepped out of her heels, grimacing in pain. My walk took me over a bridge overlooking the Deligny Pool, then along the Quai d'Orsay. I watched the Bâteaux Mouches tourist boats float up and down the river, filled to capacity. When I reached the Eiffel Tower, it must have been 6:30. Tourists with cameras, Camcorders, and Paris guidebooks milled near the base of the tower and crowded around concession stands. From the Eiffel Tower I walked to Montparnasse to see the Foyer Jeanne d'Arc, where I used to live. The nuns remembered me, nine years later. I'm home.

Place du Châtelet. Lunch at Le Mistral café. This is my first time out today and it's 4 p.m. Paris is ablaze with light under a very hot sun. It hurts the eyes. At Beaubourg (Centre Georges Pompidou), two little boys, about ten years old, break-dance to disco music. A heavyset woman with long crinkly blond hair plays a saxophone. Bushy-haired North Africans play drums and strum guitars. There are crowds everywhere on the brick-paved slope that slides down to the museum entrances. Beaubourg is like a body wearing its skeleton on the outside. It's wrapped in a long escalator that snakes upwards on the outside of the building, which makes it look as if it's always under construction.

I've had a fun few days. My legs feel like stilts from the miles of walking I've done through Paris. I'm having a great time. I met a very sweet, soft-spoken Thai government official who showed me his United Nations passport bearing a photo of himself looking adorable in a white military jacket. I also met a red-haired American guitarist who's been admitted to architecture school and plans to spend a year here supporting himself by playing guitar on the street. And I have a new buddy named Denise, an African American lawyer from Chicago. We walked and talked and laughed for hours and it turns out we know people in common. Both wearing knapsacks, we looked like sisters. We went to a jazz club called Les Trois Mallets and somehow ended up sitting with a German diplomat from Bonn who goes by the nickname "Fips." He gave us business cards and roses. Denise talked a lot and was very sociable and extroverted. I sat quietly, vaguely frightened, laughing occasionally and trying to pull myself out of myself. After a while, Fips said he wanted someone to accompany him to his car because he felt *trop paresseux*; that is, lazy. I cringed. Denise was oblivious. Fips wanted me to go. I said I'd go only if Denise went, so we both walked him up the Boulevard St.-Michel, one on each arm, probably looking like twin prostitutes. We did the cheek-kissing thing, then Denise and I ran down the block. He tooted the horn of his Mercedes (*bien sûr!*) as he drove past. Denise said, "It's always the quiet ones who arouse passion." I said that he probably chose me because I seemed passive and easily dominated. Denise said, "No big deal, you're in control." I wish I felt as confident and sure of that as she does. The next day, she and I went sightseeing all over Paris and met two gorgeous French boys in the Père-Lachaise cemetery, who looked as if they had just burst forth from puberty. They took us to Jim Morrison's grave and I got my picture taken with them. I start work tomorrow.

Work today was all right; nothing remarkable, really. I sit at a console in a large newsroom full of Europeans, who look at me with surprise. They're all English, except the head of the desk, who is American. My job is to translate and edit news copy from French to English, so it can be sent out to AFP's various subscribers.

I'm watching the opening ceremonies of the Olympic Games in L.A. on TV. I fall in and out of conflicting feelings: it's so lavish, so abundant, so obnoxiously lush and typically American . . . yet I feel pleased, too, as if I'm looking at a spoiled, bratty whiz-kid younger brother whom you love to hate but can't help liking. National pride? No, it's just that I guess I'm American, after all. Or maybe above all—at least in a foreign country.

I went to an AFP party. No other blacks. When I go to a social event I look for other black people not necessarily for company but just to gauge something about the party giver. Not that everyone should have friends from every ethnic group but it certainly says something when a person does. It was all English folks, except one annoying job-hunting American girl who said her father is an ambassador but couldn't help her get working papers. Fat, with tight red pants. I really like Risa. She's friendly and idealistic. She and her husband, Kit, are going on a year-long tour of the East and she wants to cook a meal each night and take it to a village to give to starving people. Everyone gave me trouble about not drinking. At AFP I smell a lot of alcohol on a lot of breaths. During breaks, they all have a drink (or ten) at Le Vaudeville. They have a drink after work, a drink with dinner, a drink at social gatherings. I don't like to drink unless I'm dancing, and have little tolerance for alcohol. I've always been like that. But here people think something is wrong with me, or that I'm hiding something. Risa said, "You really are the mysterious one, aren't you? Why are you so nervous about drinking? You're making me very curious. What will you do?"

"Whose language is it, anyway?" Risa laughed in answer to my comment that the English talk funny. Today, she took me on a stroll through the gardens of the Palais-Royal on our break. We had a very interesting talk about the American psyche (driven by success, money, and "that unpleasant, thrusting, ambitious, sick American culture"), the British psyche (anti-hero and anti-bourgeois, she says), poverty, the nuclear family, and my inability to step into a profession because of my family issues. She said in Britain ambition is frowned upon; wealth is discreetly played down, not lorded over poorer people the way it is in America. We talked about politics in America, Britain, and Germany (having been joined by a woman from AFP's German desk). I said Americans are the children of the world, basically self-seeking and apolitical. Risa thinks the French are the most political, then the Germans, then the Brits. Americans play Frisbee. Andrea, the German, asked us to define "political." In her view, every social conflict is political, not just the actions of governments. Risa made the point that Americans are apolitical because we have no stable working class due to the constant influx of immigrants, who eventually move from the working class to the bourgeoisie, making way for a wave of new immigrants. She said in Britain the workers have no illusions that someday they will become managers, "metaphorically win Lotto," whereas in the U.S. we are all taught the "Big Lie"— that each of us has the full opportunity to be anything and have everything, when, in fact, that is only true for actual or honorary members of the oligarchy. I don't know. I like the U.S., but we have a long way to go.

I had an interesting talk this evening with Puce and Tchoum about the harm Michael Jackson's image is spreading in the psyche of young blacks. She told me about an eighteen-year-old French West Indian who modeled himself in every detail after Michael Jackson. When his mother couldn't pay for a nose job, he committed suicide. We talked about racism throughout the world; the French call Arabs "niggers" and are increasingly supporting Jean-Marie Le Pen, the leader of France's racist National Front Party. So what must they call me? I'm beginning to realize that, in the minds of many, "Americans" are California-blond WASPs and nothing else. Blacks of all origins are the second-class citizens of the world. In every country, hatred for us grows increasingly overt. That is why so many black people hate their own blackness—they see "black" as the reason they suffer. If to be black is to be despised, then no one wants to be too black. One wants to be a Michael Jackson-style "different," meaning "better," black. That's sick, but we're all racially sick in America. Bert said I see everything in black and white. Well, it is—at least, when you're black. A white person should just go through one day of the glances, bad vibes, put-downs, and slights we black people endure each day. Maybe they cannot comprehend something so outside of their collective experience. White means privilege in this world, and privilege acts as a blinder.

I am blown away. Chez Puce I met a Dominican bean pole Rastafari tall as a skyscraper. He let me touch his dreadlocks, which he usually keeps under a cloth hat to "protect" them. For three hours he preached the Rasta doctrine, smoking joint after joint with Puce and Tchoum, in a lively patchwork-quilt language mixing French, English, and Creole, all ungrammatical. He's very striking and engaging, a musician who calls himself "a spy in Babylon." I vacillated between two attitudes. "He's a man, watch out, be careful, where's my knife?" and "This is a very spiritual person and I like him." Puce laughed all night because he kept trying to rap to me, but not in an aggressive, offensive way, but rather, "This sister, she just like her voice" (he said I had a nice voice). He loves his Rasta stuff. All night long I heard "Oh, Jah!" and "Jah love." His holy trinity is Haile Selaissie, Marcus Garvey, and Bob Marley, Marley being a sort of Christ figure. Tchoum told scary stories about voodoo and people in trances. He said, "The white man goes to Africa, he sees buildings, people, clothing, but he doesn't see *l'Afrique profonde*." He and the Rasta laughed and gave each other high-fives, as if they know secrets others don't. We listened to gospel music that I brought from home and to reggae. I looked at us: a Dominican, a Guadeloupian, an African, an American, all black, originally from the same place centuries ago. When I meet a black person in Paris, their language, accent, and style of dress immediately tell me who enslaved or colonized their ancestors. We're different only because of our cultures.

This afternoon, I met four African Americans near Le Vaudeville. Two military couples stationed in Germany. I was so happy to see regular niggers like me. I walked up to them as if toward a vision and asked "Are you *American?*" "Like corn bread and peas," came the answer. We all went inside and drank beer (the men) and hot chocolate (the women). It was very enjoyable.

I visited the *Newsweek* Paris office. I wanted to meet Michael Lerner, son of Alan Jay Lerner, a millionaire Broadway producer or some shit. Michael has a very straight nose, big attractive eyes, and a phony and irritating persona. He's shorter than me, ha! While mouthing nonsense about how interesting I found my experience at *Newsweek* New York, I was secretly resenting the spoiled Harvard bastard who never spent a day as a researcher because of his name. I talked to Fred Coleman, the head of the office, who said they didn't need anyone right now, but to check back every once in a while.

Another day that began unfortunately with a nightmare. I was walking outside, in front of Paulette, and she jokingly grabbed my crotch from behind. I turned around laughing only to find that it was a black guy who had grabbed me. I was shocked and terrified. He raped me.

Last night, I met this twenty-six-year-old from Chicago named Melinda who said that the night before last an Arab attacked her when she was going into the Fondation des Etat-Unis dormitory at Cité Université. She said he pinned her to the floor, shouting, "Je suis un arabe!" and "jacking off" on her. She's big, too, taller and broader than me. It scared her horribly and she was still pretty depressed last night. I volunteered in all seriousness to help her find and kill him, but she's going back to Chicago in a couple of days. If she'd had my switchblade it might have made a difference. I bought her some beers and tried to cheer her up.

Lately, my head has been full of thoughts on the comparative quality of life in Paris and New York. Paris feels scaled down and slightly inefficient but eminently human. I feel I could actually *live* here, have a quiet, small, sane life without agonizing over "success." These Europeans are full of life, not ambition. I was visiting Lainie, one of the Brits at AFP, and we talked about it. She was horrified to hear about the American obsession with winners and losers, the quest to be number one, the best, the brightest, the most highly paid. She finds it all strange. I told her about the cutthroat competitiveness of the Ivy League college system, the scramble for bylines at *Newsweek*, how any self-respecting law student should be firmly entrenched in a career by thirty. She frowned, then laughed. "Who would want to be firmly entrenched in some boring career anyway?" she asked, cuddling Fellini, her butterscotch-colored cat. Lainie said she's happy right where she is. "I like my apartment, my job, and my cat. I don't need to be the boss." I'm in acute conflict. I would like to live here because it's so manageable and so sane, despite everything. There is less pressure. Stores close in the middle of the day for two-hour lunch breaks, restaurants shut down for a month-long holiday in the summer, waiters and waitresses are slow . . . it's all inconvenient, yes, but it reflects an attitude about life and work, about priorities. I'm not saying Europeans aren't ambitious, after all, Europe colonized half the planet, but it's different. In Paris, I can sink into a com-

fortable oblivion; never get my face on the cover of *People* magazine or sell 30 million copies of an album or make partner at a
Wall Street law firm and still feel okay. Much of my anger stems
from the American life-style, the conditioned need to be at the
apex of everything to feel like you're worth anything. To be Michael Jackson—dazzlingly talented, shockingly wealthy, eternally
young, amazingly pure, appealingly androgynous. I feel that is the
impossible dream we Americans are taught to strive for, to be the
Michael Jackson of law, of journalism, of medicine, of business, of
crime, of insanity. And look what a nightmare *he's* living.

Risa and I hung out in the Palais-Royal gardens on our break. She
said in Britain you are pegged right away by your accent rather
than what school you went to, and is ashamed of her upper-crust
accent and background. She refused to go to university, became a
journalist at nineteen, and married at twenty-two. "I was raised in
what they call stockbroker country," she moaned. Enrolled at a
posh boarding school for "young ladies" alongside the kids of diplomats, she was thrown out for leaving the premises without per-
mission, much to her parents' shame and dismay. Much of what
she is about is rebellion against her family and background. But
she can't lose the accent and still carries it like a burden. "It's
really bad because even if you want to get involved in trade-union
stuff, people hear the accent and are hostile." She collects money
for striking mine workers and traveled throughout India for a year.
It's fascinating to me to learn how people I would assume to have
it made also struggle with issues of family and background.

My AFP internship is coming to an end. I would like to stay on
here because I'm the first black intern, but, fuck it, I'm going the
hell home. Too bad I have to go back, but I feel like my life is
there—Bert, my friends, my cat, law school, school loans, the
McDonalds, subway thugs, a knife in my pocket and gun in my

waistband, being fucked up. I don't want my stay here to end but I want to be in New York. What to do? I've certainly learned a lot at AFP but it isn't the most exciting job around, translating and rewriting news copy. New York is dirt, screeching subway wheels, terror, tension, major depressions, minor pleasures, envy, emptiness, poverty, emotional suffering, brutality, rape, worry, competition, rage, acting out, crying and crying and crying, and finally suicide. Not much there. But Bert. Therapy has really made a dent in my hard head. Of course, it's easy to feel healthy in Paris, but that's exactly how I feel, like I am a little better.

Yesterday, Risa and I talked about the insidious corrupting effects of middle-class living. I think that's why I refuse to become a middle-class professional, because I've always hated them. In the black middle class, people try to outbourgeois the bourgeois. Suddenly, just by virtue of your economic circumstances, your attitudes and values change for the worse. Already, most of my friends are lawyers, bankers, doctors, and law students, just because of the schools I've attended. But not me—as long as I'm not one of them, I'm okay. Risa said middle class is a state of mind and that one should be vigilant and not succumb to the seductive lure of materialism. Then we discussed Angela Davis's bourgeois background, which didn't inhibit her political development.

That's it, I'm off to study law. The plane has pierced the cloud bank and I'm en route to New York. I don't regret having left New York and I don't regret leaving Paris. All is well.

New York: September 1984–February 1985

It's going to be a formidable year at NYU. I'm emotionally and physically worn out from my return to law school. Went home tonight to see the family. Not too depressing. Ann, as usual, told me about the drugs available. Mother, as usual, told me who died.

I registered for Beginning Bengali at Columbia so I can see Bert this year. I'm back from my first week of school and everything looks great. I feel good. I've gone to all four of my courses and intellectually none will pose a problem. Also, I'm working on changing my attitudes, rechanneling my thoughts. When "hot dogs" show off in class, I'm not thrown into a fury as before. I grab my thoughts firmly by the wrist and tug them away from envy, competition, insecurity, and unrealistic expectations of myself. All these tendencies of mine and, more important, their deleterious effect on my health, were brought home to me very clearly by Bert. So now I say to myself, Janet, you're not him, he's not you. There is no relation between the two of you; his "more" isn't automatically your "less." In general, I have pulled my antennae in. When a student said, referring to the fires, "Well, you certainly made something of a splash here before, ha-ha," it upset me, but I didn't plot her murder; rather, I let the feeling float off.

NYU is getting to me. I'm trying hard to be cool and mellow but I feel rage bubbling and seeping whenever a guard stops me or glances my way. Every "How're you doing?" sounds laden with suspicion and accusation. This morning I saw that bastard Dr. Block. I hate him. He's a typical smug shrink. "You seem angry," he observed. "How can I help you?" I gave him the royal piss-off treatment. "You can't. I'm here to fulfill the conditions of my agreement with NYU." "Well, I'm here, the Service is here. If you need long-term therapy I can refer you . . ." "Not that disaster again. Coming here last time was a catastrophe. What I remember about you is you telling me 'You're going to end up in jail or in a hospital. Bye, Miss McDonald.' Do you remember saying that?" "Uh, no. Unless it's out of context." I said, "You blocked it out."

What a glib jerk! He said he would talk to Bert about making other arrangements, since I don't want to see him. "What is your therapist's specialty? Psychiatrist? Psychologist?" "I don't know. We haven't discussed her credentials." "Well, what does she have after her name?" "A blank." As I was leaving he mumbled, "Welcome back." I grunted and walked out, wanting to blow up the world. I know Dr. Dumbo is going to tell Dean Rawls I was hostile. I just want to get out of school with my J-D degree. Rage is pulling at my thoughts, mingling in my mood. Rape trial, fire marshals, assholish friends, inept family, jail cells, and prostitutes. And people expect me to walk around with more than a fake smile and a phony hello? Fuck you! I am angry and full of hatred and violence. It seems like everything started spiraling uncontrollably downwards after the rape. It devastated me and I have remained so. I'm in a Thanatos mood.

How do you spell "fucking headache"? B-E-R-T. Second session: "This isn't an emergency room. Would it be too much of a burden to ask you to limit our interactions to the weekly sessions?" She depressed me. What are therapists for, if not to help you through emergencies?

School is good but things are getting thicker and denser. There's a lot of work, a lot of things to do outside of schoolwork like look for a job and try to get on a journal, but not enough time. I'm spent at the day's end. Paulette said she can tell I'm happy to be back in law school. I am. I like the analysis and intellectualism that law study requires. My teachers are brilliant and my own powers of analysis dull in comparison, but I am delighted nonetheless.

Nightmare. A woman was in the hall at Mother's apartment holding a silver gun. She said, "I'm not going to shoot anybody." *Bang!* She shot me in the chest. Everything went black as I fell, my chest stinging. I heard another shot as I hit the floor. Still conscious, I wondered whether she had shot me again, or someone else. My mouth was filling with blood. As I lay dying, I was very sad, thinking, "I can't believe it's over—and right in the middle of law school." I awoke with a stinging sensation in my chest, feeling depressed.

Next week I plan to send out twenty letters to try to get a summer associate-job offer for next summer. I'm going to send one to Floyd Abrams, although I doubt his firm will take me.

I was up at Columbia today to see Bert and ran into Fred Friendly, the former CBS president who was my teacher at the J-School. I remember how he shocked us all on the first day of class by recounting how, a couple of years earlier, a black student stood up in class while Friendly was praising the Founding Fathers and their Constitution. The student said, "What are you talking about? To Thomas Jefferson, the black man was just a nigger!" A stunned murmur rolled across the classroom, then we had a lively discussion about the Constitution. Anyway, Friendly shook my hand and congratulated me for having graduated from journalism school. I told him I lost my little blue copy of the U.S. Constitution and he immediately gave me another one. I think he walks around with a bunch in his pocket. Friendly is a great person. His hand trembled as it reached for mine—age.

Bert upset me with her female-slave routine of "They're not all bad," meaning men, and her suggestion that I'm paranoid. She said I'm constantly reliving the atrocities I've suffered. If she thinks she's going to lure me into accepting the rape she might as well forget it. The only self-respect a rape victim (or survivor, whatever) has stems from her anger and quest for revenge. Fuck "I'm okay, the rapist's okay."

I learned in Criminal Procedure class that those pigs from the Secret Service violated every constitutional protection against unreasonable searches and seizures. A strip search under those circumstances was outrageous. Where was the "probable cause" or "reasonable articulable suspicion"? I'm so angry. Also, the fire marshals' behavior in my room was coercive and my "confession" never would have withstood a legal challenge.

The police are looking for Jean's latest boyfriend in connection with a murder that was committed in Mother's building early this morning; they even searched Mother's apartment. The most horrible thing about it is that two kids were in the victim's apartment when it happened. Jean's afraid there might be a revenge killing —of her—so she wants to move her two daughters and the boyfriend to Iowa. That's pretty stupid, aiding and abetting. She really knows how to pick 'em. As poor Mother said, "Nothin' but mess, mess and more mess." Maybe I *should* go to Paris.

Allison Klein, the woman who runs the Karate School for Women, said a ten-year-old girl in the kids' karate class fought off an attempted rape by screaming, the way she'd been taught in class, timing it just right. The guy followed her into a building, took her to the basement at knife point, pulled off her panties, and threw her down on the floor. The girl screamed and scared him off. Allison had all of us scream "Utz!" She said that women are often too inhibited to scream to save their lives. I didn't scream with the rest of the class. I was choking on depression, so I just pretended. Maybe I should have screamed at Cornell and saved *my*self. I don't know how to scream, actually. The woman next to me said she had been raped at gunpoint and that learning karate was making her feel more powerful. I'm only a white belt and know deep down that I'll never be able to fight *him* off if he finds me. These wounded women, like me, are deluding themselves. I said nothing and felt low-energy and ashamed. I don't want people to know that Janet the cool MENSA jokester was raped.

A couple of nights ago, I had one of my apocryphal, symbolic dreams. I am sitting in a very plush expensive restaurant in the lobby of the new AT&T building with the building's architect, an older, elegant Frenchman. We are drinking a fine wine. I'm wearing jeans and sneakers and initially have trouble getting past the waiters, until they discover I am with the "monsieur." The wine rushes to my head and I nearly fall off my chair, greatly embarrassed. The "monsieur" and other "beautiful people" at our table are not fazed by my gaucheness. Suddenly there is a shootout on the street and the police are chasing someone who is running from an armored car. My blood races with the excitement of impending violence. I rush outside and find myself in a ghetto, low tenement buildings and projects looming nearby. The streets are crowded with project people running toward the excitement. I, too, am excited and feel a sort of catharsis as I breathe the dead air of ghetto life. I jump into a vehicle and head down a long, dark street toward the projects. Around me, there is danger and agitation: I feel I'm going home. Suddenly I turn around and drive back to the restaurant. The "beautiful people" are still there and accept my absence as they accepted my near-fall off the chair. This was the kind of "two worlds" dream I've had a number of times.

I got a bullshit letter from Floyd Abrams's law firm claiming it is "policy" not to hire former staff in attorney positions. So why is there a big-busted Brit who was a paralegal with me working there as an associate right now? The only difference between us, besides about three bra sizes, is the fact that her father is the chairman of British Petroleum. As the world turns. Fuck them. Underwood & Hansen has offered me a position as a summer associate. I'll be making more than $850 a week! I was flabbergasted, thrilled, dancing on my toes. Then came the crisis. I'm headed toward being a corporate lawyer making an unseemly amount of money. Why should I make twice as much money a week as my mother gets in a month? It's a sellout, a whitewash. I don't want to become bourgeois, materialistic, selfish. People are miserable everywhere, suffering because the evil and corrupt corporations I will be serving lust for greater profits. If Underwood & Hansen makes me an offer of permanent employment at the end of the summer, I will be paid $50,000 a year. It's not fair but that is the system. Yet I don't want to work again as a $12,000 a year paralegal and feel humiliated, pitied, and condescended to. That, too, is the system. The more money one earns, the more one is treated like a human being. It makes me want to cry. I will be aligning myself with oppressors, elitists, and snobs who would look at every McDonald with fear and loathing. But part of me wants to feel superior, powerful, and important. And since my fundamental values are screwed (I *am* American, after all) the only way for me to feel that I am worthy is to lock myself behind pin-striped bars in a steel-and-glass skyscraper and rub shoulders with the worst preppy snots Ivy Leaguedom has produced. I have had to make myself Superblackwoman just to get a job that a less dazzling white student would get easily. A Master's degree in journalism, internships at *Newsweek* and the Agence France-Presse, Vassar, Cornell, Columbia, Paris, Floyd Abrams as a reference. They should make me God! But do I want to be where I am going? I wanted to write novels, grow dreadlocks, live in Paris, revolt. Why do I have to be a fucking successful, tormented lawyer? It's called the reality principle. Mother is proud, my project people are proud, thus I am proud. Everyone in my family needs money and no one has any, or the potential to get any, except me. I have no choice. Shit, I don't want to be a sellout Madison Avenue nerd. I wanna be in jail without bail from a broken home in Spanish Harlem, a bullet lodged in my side from a gang fight I had years ago, muscular and track-marked, wearing

black Lees and untied sneakers, full of righteous hatred and justi-
fiable anger, guilt- and conscience-free, full of shit, a rat in a maze,
a violent jerk. But alive, with a perverse sort of integrity.

I feel like something is tearing apart inside me. Tears fall. In one
week, two women have been killed by men during an attempted
rape and robbery, respectively. One white, young, privileged;
the other, black, older, poor. It sickens me. Caroline Eisenberg,
twenty-three years old and just out of Harvard. It happened around
106th Street and West End Avenue. She fought desperately,
screaming for help, but died after bleeding on a rooftop for six
hours. Neighbors heard the screams and called the police, then sat
and listened to her die. Why couldn't anyone run up to the roof
with a club or anything? I would have—he would have had to kill
two people. The other woman lived in the Gowanus projects in
Brooklyn. She was beaten in the courtyard and then shot. Her
neighbors didn't respond right away, and when they did, the police
were slow to show up. It makes me feel angry, impotent, depressed,
and vulnerable.

The police caught the vermin who killed Caroline—the fucking
idiot son of the building's super. The son said, "It was her fault."
I cried all day. I had often walked around the neighborhood where
it happened, hunting the killer. I figured I'd see it in his eyes, then
kill him. This is war.

Christmas. I got a guitar from Paulette. Kevin gave me a card in
which he wrote, "Thank you for everything you've ever done for
me since the first time you carried me on your shoulders." I was
extremely touched. Ann was taking heroin in the bathroom and
left her little drug-filled purse on the dirty clothes hamper. I found
it and gave it to her. She offered me some but I refused.

Fell asleep thinking that certain people forfeit their humanity through their barbarous actions and may be treated accordingly—buried alive. Fantasized about burying my rapist alive. Only four more days until exams.

I studied six to ten hours a day every day, for each exam, and now they're over! I'm done! I've been feeling great all day.

Jean said last Sunday somebody pulled a .22 on Kevin and tried to take his gold chain. Fuck! It scared me so bad. Young black men really are an endangered species, but unlike other threatened species, the danger comes from within. Should anything happen to Kevin I'm going to become a serial killer.

Yesterday evening, I had an unpleasant dinner with two law students. I ate too slowly and was awkward and quiet (until I told my stupid anecdote about having a mouthful of fish bones during my Underwood & Hansen interview lunch). I'm sure I seemed like a flake. Veiled insults directed at me were plentiful: "You're taking Agency? I thought only future Wall Street flunkies took Agency." "Oh, you're in the Women and the Law course? It's full of liberals who aren't even going to the Women and the Law Conference." "Oh, you made the *Review of Law and Social Change*, the journal that everyone and their brother is on?" Ann Marie may denigrate my journal (probably because she's not on *any* of the school's five journals) but it means a great deal to me that I'm finally on one. My first try at Cornell was preempted by the rape, and my subsequent unsuccessful attempt at NYU probably fed into my acting out with the fires. A lot of people would've already given up. I hung in there. Still, I felt pretty down by the time I got home.

At a party in the East Village I met a twenty-two-year-old writer from Yale named David Leavitt whose coming-out-to-Mother novel was favorably reviewed in *The New York Times*. There also was a youthful-looking black Columbia law professor who was gay, out, and cool. He said, "I'm uptown, and available to all progressive law students." I was impressed and slightly intimidated, and hung out in the bathroom with another recent Yale grad who writes for *The Village Voice*. She's been disowned by her famous black radical father because she is half white. What a joke! *He* marries a white woman, fathers two kids, then rejects the kids because they're biracial. It depressed me to be around so many of my peers doing what I only dream about. I went home burdened by the thought that I am a loser.

Friday, I attended my very first MENSA gathering, hoping to meet bright people and widen my social horizons. I ended up dining with an odd group of people at a small Greek restaurant on Fifteenth Street. My fellow MENSAns: a couple of retired high-school teachers who talked about cars and taxes; a fat, middle-aged guy ranting about his boss's million-dollar yacht; and an aging peacock with blue eyeliner and pink lipstick where lips should have been, screaming in a strong Brooklyn accent something totally stupid about Freud's "hydraulic theory—you know, the superego, the id, and the ego." When they started laughing about penis envy versus breast envy and telling jokes about seasickness ("If you get seasick, the first thing you should do is sit under a tree"), I realized that intelligence-quotient tests must measure something other than intelligence. Perhaps they simply measure one's ability to score well on intelligence-quotient tests.

America's corporate structure, i.e., capitalist profit-motive system, is responsible for each and every individual moment of suffering in this country and beyond—people without shelter freezing to death, people dying of diseases and drug addiction, women suffering abuse, Bernard Goetz's teenage victim Darrell Cabey, Ann on drugs . . . If I choose to serve the corporations that create and perpetuate these injustices, I am *personally* responsible for all the anguish and misery of America's poor, America's underclass, America's niggers of all races. How can I do that when I'm one of them? It's wrong. No wonder I haven't gone to classes in weeks; I languish in bed in horror, the blankets over my head. I spoke to Bert this morning about some of this. She says I'm "on a conveyor belt to corporate death" and that I need to explore other options. "I can't," I said. "I've been to the mountaintop." "And found a crater," she retorted. At least we manage to laugh.

Bert stopped me from sending an angry letter to Floyd Abrams about the summer-job rejection.

Fall semester grades are posted and I got four B's! My insides shriek with joy. Maybe next semester I can get an A in something. Paulette said, "Imagine if you really went to school and studied—you'd get straight A's. You study one week and get B's." She's right, but who has the peace of mind for that?

February 1985–June 1986

I realize why I keep renewing my membership in that absurd society MENSA. Blacks and IQ's have a troubled history and I want to be a living reminder to "others" that a black person can also have a high IQ.

I'm not straightening my hair this summer for my job at Underwood & Hansen. I talked it over with another black woman law student and we decided it would be degrading.

I am in a troubled state. I sacrificed it all today and impulsively applied for a senior editorial-board position at the *Review of Law and Social Change*—after weighing all the pros and cons and coming up with all cons. Why? Because the other black journal members were very disappointed when I said I wanted only an ordinary editorial position (and I didn't even really want that!). "Only that?!" Qualasia asked, suggesting I apply to be co-editor, as she intends to do. Me, co-editor? Is she nuts? It is obvious she doesn't know me. (Do I feel a headache arriving?) Haynes also complained about my choice. "We need more of us at the top so we can get more minorities on the journal next year. The whites don't want us in positions of power." I told him I didn't feel qualified for the top position. "That's a crock of shit," he declared. Later I talked to Faust, a friend who works in the law library. She understood perfectly the misery of being swept into the world of "we need a black woman" symbolism. The same thing happened to her at a women's meeting at Yale where she was the only black. One woman said, "It would be good to get a black woman to speak," and all eyes turned on Faust, who looked toward the ceiling for divine inspiration. Bert is right—this is all another form of tokenism, a dehumanization whereby one is reduced to a politically correct skin color or relevant gender. And I went for it. What an ass! But wouldn't it be great if I *were* capable emotionally, psychologically, and intellectually of being on the board. What a comeback that would be! Lena Horne on Broadway! I'd feel elated and victorious. But can I do it? I can't even make it from one day to the next without plunging into some fugue state. Maybe I'll be in shape when the time comes.

Nightmare. I was walking with my nieces and Daddy along a beach. The water grabbed me around the waist and began pulling me away from land. Daddy and a few onlookers watched indifferently. I tried to swim against the powerful waves, since I wasn't that far from shore yet, but my thin arms were weak and ineffective. The undertow was mighty and dragged me farther out. I grabbed hold of a steel beam upright in the water, screaming, "No, no! I will not be swept away!" I clung to the beam, with nothing solid under my feet and unable to swim.

Amazing! I am so psyched. Ever since yesterday, I have been feeling cheerful. No more sense of loss of control of my external life and internal experience. I am convinced all this has to do with Bert talking to me, the effect of which was manifested in that incredible dream I had where I fought being swept out to sea. Bert makes me feel that I can be strong and resist Thanatos.

Yesterday, Bert said I am light-years ahead of where I was last year, that I'm beginning to understand my envy and to see how it messes me up and leads to Thanatos. She said what therapy does is surround this systemic *thing* I have like an antibiotic, then shrink and ultimately destroy it. But I must watch out for little baby bacteria that may escape. And if they do, I mustn't panic. Could it really be happening? I don't want to get my hopes up. Bert sounds psyched, though—it's obvious she really believes I'm on my way. I wonder what it would feel like to be all right.

How awkward—Qualasia and I are applying for the same editorial-board position. My interview is Friday. Do I really want to do that shit? Nope. But I desperately want to feel special. Unfortunately, envious thoughts slip into my mind when I see a student who is bright in class and who probably has straight A's.

I was interviewed by the senior board today: "Why didn't you apply for editor in chief?" I said, "Well, I was intimidated. I'll apply to be Jesus, but I don't know if I can be God." Everybody laughed.

Bert and I talked about the rapist and the appellate opinion confirming his conviction, which now, of course, is moot since he got out of prison anyway. Nevertheless, the opinion still torments me, like a burr in my skin. The dissenting judge criticized me for failing to scream, assuming, I guess, that I was in a populated dorm. If he had checked his facts he would've known classes hadn't begun and the dorm was almost empty. What an ass, the Honorable Judge Marr. He sits in his judicial chambers, some old white guy, analyzing and judging how I responded in a situation where a psychopath with a lethal hatred of black women is threatening to beat me over the head. He concludes that "the requirement of earnest resistance, not met here, involves a duty to . . ." blah, blah, blah. It's enraging, infuriating. I'd give anything to be able to arrange an exchange whereby Judge Marr would be raped and I would sit smugly and decide that, no, the requisite elements of resistance simply were not met under the dictates of the Model Penis Code.

The journal editor in chief just called to offer me the Senior Note and Comment Editor position on the board. I accepted. Hey, I'm on top of the dung heap! I'm the Boss! Me and Bruce Springsteen! (It will probably be a pain in the ass.) Qualasia wasn't offered a position. Unfuckingbelievable. Maybe the universe has decided I've had enough rejection and suffering. Thank you.

Yesterday at school I was a star! Everyone was congratulating me and shaking my hand for being offered a position on the board. But now the thrill has worn off and dull dread has set in. Long ass day today has taken its toll; I'm drained.

Dean Rawls said to me on the street today, "Congratulations on the journal position." They *are* watching me. I felt weird but glad, too. Slowly but surely I am redeeming myself. I even forgive Rawls. He wasn't trying to hurt me, he just made a bad decision. Now that NYU has taken me back, that past doesn't matter.

As part of my comeback I got up at 8:30 and shampooed the rug before starting my massive study program! On Easter no one was home but Ann. She tried to rip me off again, claiming a "friend" had a brand-new .25 automatic for sale for $160. I said, "Like the other one?" referring to another time she said the same thing and kept the money I'd given her. How could she do that to me, rip off her own sister? I didn't give her a penny.

I am freaked out! I just left Jean's boyfriend Arkeem, who is wanted by the police for the murder in Mother's building. He brought me a derringer "for self-defense." It is worth $200 but he accepted $20. Not only is he a bright vegetarian, he's actually nice! This was the first time I ever talked to him at any length. I wanted to hate him but I can't, because he didn't rape. In fact, he talked a lot about how he "hates that shit" and lectures Jean's daughters about protecting themselves. Something he saw on the news particularly outraged him; a three-year-old girl was raped by a middle-aged "fat, flabby Caucasian." He said he'd shoot him—"wouldn't be no calling the police." He knows so much about survival, what to do if you're busted. Compared to him, I am naïve, bookwormish, and have no common sense, just like Mother and Daddy used to say. He would never have confessed to setting fires or cried on a cop's shoulder. What will Bert say? I feel outrage at his act but am enamored of the safety I feel with him. He would never have to see a therapist, because he's totally grounded. And he knows the law better than I do. We talked about how I should handle situations where I'm accosted: You shoot at the right side of the body, "to maim," then claim self-defense. We were at the Fourteenth Street subway stop when I saw two cops approaching. I tensed. Arkeem didn't flinch. Looking straight ahead, he said, "Just take my arm like we're boyfriend and girlfriend," and we walked right past them, just another young black couple. I was shaking. When we reached my building he stood at the outer door and wouldn't leave until I had checked my apartment, come back out, and waved to him. I'm confused. I felt safe with him—a killer. But why did he kill? He referred to it in passing as his "little problem." I had dehumanized and labeled him a killer, an animal, a madman, an object to be loathed. And now his humanity disconcerts me. He is just a person, like me, only one who has killed. But what did I expect, Mr. Hyde? He was very protective of me and said that if anyone hounds me I should tell him and he'll "take care of it." No one ever said anything that kind to me. He's strong, powerful, unafraid. He would never be raped.

Bert can't relate to my rage and fear because she has been lucky, spared. I don't think she has ever been raped. I'm glad that she hasn't been. Some guy raped three women yesterday on the East Side between Sixteenth and Eighteenth Streets. I feel quite frightened and vulnerable since I have not gone to the gym or to karate class in months. I could not survive another rape—it would kill me, whether the rapist did or not. I wish I could undo it somehow, only *that* would release me. But as it stands, once raped, always raped. It's gun-toting time. Wore it for the first time to see Bert; *she* was wearing little black-and-purple rain boots. The contrast made me feel distant. Our realities are so different. I want so much from her but end up feeling the same isolation, alienation, and otherworldliness I feel with everyone else. Why does she talk about Arkeem so much? It bothers her I think that, as she puts it, I make an exception for him because of my "feelings of awe" about his "power."

It's already May. I took the Evidence exam yesterday. It lasted two hours. I knew very little, just enough to fill a large thimble, having skipped classes, not read the materials, and only barely studied for the exam. But I'm sure I passed and that's all that matters on a pass-fail exam. That was my final Final. I am thoroughly happy and delighted to have just completed a full year of law school rather successfully. In two weeks, I start my summer law job as a corporate yuppie clown.

I just watched a film on Channel 13 about a black Vietnam vet. It was powerful. Bert kept coming to mind. Not Bert the Beloved Shrink, but a white woman named Doris Bertocci who knows nothing of rap music or dreadlocks or Prince, all of which is forgivable (she *is* white, after all). But I wonder, how can she feel me, truly empathize with my pain and confusion, much of which has to do with the visceral experience of race and class. That perspective must also be brought to the psychological inquiry. Damaged psyches are formed in individuals by their world; in my case, a black, poor, ghetto world. Can Bert truly know any of this? I don't know. I wish she weren't so very white; black things seem foreign to her, especially poor black things, or, rather, things of the black poor. Sometimes I feel that if she weren't so hopelessly and perhaps resolutely white she could understand me more. For example, when I say I feel the obligation to help out my family, yes, it has to do with my own "aristocratic" noblesse-oblige guilt, having been the privileged one, and yes, I probably get a masochistic martyr's pleasure from it, and yes, I deny and kill off myself in proportion to how much I serve them, but it's more than that. It is based on the larger recognition that Society is no longer willing to help people like my family. I cannot abandon them. That's something I doubt Bert has ever had to worry about regarding her family. She has the luxury of independence, selfhood, and mental health. The psychological dynamic is altogether different for a poor, black person. But when others say, "Get a good job and help your family," that triggers in me images of the house nigger, the bourgeois Negro, the black yuppie, identities that make me recoil. How much of myself must I sell in order to buy my family's financial security? Can a white person who is very white help a fucked-up black person in a fucked-up racist culture? Probably not. But Dr. Gaines didn't help much either, and she's black.

Shopped all day for lawyer clothes. Bought two suits and three shirts. Painful.

Well, I'm done with shopping, having found the Perfect Shoe at Maxime's. I have some lovely outfits to wear to work and a leather briefcase in which I'll carry *The New York Times* and my Frisbee. Perhaps because of the prospect of wearing grownup, power-broker outfits and being called a "summer associate" I am beginning to feel psyched. I mean, gosh, it is exciting, especially for me, the Fuck-up Kid. Little by little I'm scrambling out of the pit, regaining my natural position atop the dung heap. Soon, instead of being benevolently pitied, I will be viciously envied. Life is so meaningful, isn't it?

Underwood & Hansen is a WASP firm. Bink Rothberg said she doesn't like WASPs, "except to bed with occasionally." She is Jewish and is going to a Jewish firm. There are no black firms, so black law students have to like either WASPs or Jews. High school taught me to appreciate Jews, but arrogant, robber baron, silver-spoon-sucking flaxen-haired blondes from split-level homes will do just fine, too. There *is* something comforting about a people who absolutely will not pee in the shower and stand for the principles that it's okay, even noble, to live life as a corporate flunky, that it's okay to be selfish and tastefully greedy, that being a snot is good, not bad.

Beat. Slightly bummed. First day of work at my summer law-firm job. Everyone was nice but I must admit I felt very insecure and scared. Had lunch with two Jewish associates who were demoralized and talked cattily about Jewish weddings. Met a friendly black

woman associate, the only black lawyer there, who introduced herself as "Wanda Jones, Harvard '83."

I have been working at Underwood & Hansen for a month and I
am dully unhappy. So this is the summer associate mountaintop,
a lucrative firm job in a prestigious corporate-law firm where disease is palpable? People are driven and hyper. I can't even read
through a whole case because I'm instantly bored. I feel dumb. I'm
working longer hours than any other associate and yet get nothing
done. Today I went to the firm's obligatory Friday afternoon
"happy hour" (they should call it "depressed hour"). I was giggling
in a corner with cute Peter Arnold from NYU when the only
woman partner, Mary McInerney, Harvard '64, came over. She has
a large, ruddy face and an exhausting handshake. "We haven't
met. I'm Mary McInerney." Trying to seem interested, I asked her
about her practice. "I *love* the practice of law, I just *love* litigating!"
We chatted for ten painful minutes until she said, "Well . . ." and
I said, "Yes . . ." and we both flew off in opposite directions.

Today I went to lunch with the black associate, a distressingly
cocky young thing, who had arranged for us to meet up with her
best friend, Cynthia, also Harvard '83. I hate going out with two
best friends. They both have shoulder-length permed hair that they
have done at Saks. My hair suddenly felt short and scraggly. In
addition, all twenty of their combined perfectly filed and polished
fingernails were also done at Saks. I slipped my hands onto my lap
to hide my chewed cuticles and short nails. They talked shop—
papers filed, pre-trial motions, commodities work. Wanda had just
successfully argued some motion in court and was gloating. I
smiled, comprehending nothing. They wear eye makeup and a
touch of lipstick, and are gorgeous and confident. I felt ugly and
tongue-tied, so I laughed a lot: "Ha, ha! Really?! Ha, ha, ha! That's
amazing!" Did I laugh too loud? Of course I did. They discussed

the upcoming Harvard black-alumni bash. "NYU" sounds so pale in comparison. It doesn't even have a real name, just initials.

A few nights ago an old, black, drunken derelict saw me standing at the West Fourth Street token booth in my suit and said to his equally wretched companion, "That's a black white girl." At first I laughed, then I felt pissed and said, "Fuck you, you fucking zombie-ass drunken bastard."

Two good, no, great things happened. I got an A in Women and the Law! My first A in law school. And the head of the summer associate program said a memo I did for him was "a good piece of work." I blushed with joy.

June 11, 1985, 10:30 p.m. I'm sick and numb, emptied out and dazed. A letter from Albany, Department of Law. I picked up the letter at Mother's and thought initially that it was a job offer. I opened it on the way home and cried a little on the train. I felt my head explode and my stomach implode. The rapist is suing the State of New York for wrongful prosecution since the State was obligated to release him from prison because the Ithaca prosecutor wouldn't retry the rape case. He wants twenty million dollars for destroying my life. Larry Zimmerman is the assistant district attorney defending New York State and in his letter asks for my "help." The breath left me when I read the letter. I have to kill him. I'll go to prison, maybe forever. Should I ask Arkeem? It's horrifying that this ordeal won't ever, ever end. I must make it go away by making *him* go away. I don't want to end up in prison but I can't go through this again without striking back. He has already hurt me so much.

The other evening, I dined and cocktailed with the Underwood & Hansen lawyers, distracted by memories of the rape and trial. At one point, I had a mental break; I was talking to a senior associate when all of a sudden his face was enormous, the most prominent thing in the room. I felt myself staring at him in silence, words evaporating in my mouth. I don't know if he noticed. I'm not going to get a job offer anyway, so fuck it. I have this shit to deal with.

Saw Bert but was in so much pain that in the beginning I just sat there. She looked concerned and said, "You seem subdued." Dead is more like it, I thought. Eventually, I was able to tell her the bad news. She was utterly disgusted by his lawsuit but her words of support couldn't reach me. Nothing could. Last night, I fell asleep crying and was crying again soon after waking. Do I want to keep living? I manage to make my mouth smile, my legs walk, I say words, do research, but inside I sit quietly crying all day. This latest shock makes me want to die, but if I do, I swear it won't be alone.

I feel blank inside. School has resumed but I'm falling behind in my schoolwork and class attendance. Too burdened.

I got an offer of a permanent job at Underwood & Hansen after I graduate. The hiring partner said, "We'd like to welcome you to the Underwood & Hansen family." Surreal. Then it was off to a Chinese restaurant, where I had an uncomfortable "wish-I-were-under-the-table" celebratory lunch with three partners, who strained to make conversation with me and, failing, eventually relaxed into talking about golf among themselves. I guess I'll go there if I can't get a better offer but I don't really like the firm. Most of the young associates are miserable, and worse, the firm's on the wrong side in the Agent Orange litigation.

Homicide fills my thoughts. I can't take being picked apart once more by a rapist's lawyers. At work, I play the role of the black upper-class WASP—it takes me out of myself somewhat. But I'm in so much pain. I have no appetite because of this depression and weigh only 112 pounds, the least I've weighed in years. Work is okay but I find it hard to concentrate. Bert is putting me through hell (I'm sure she's writing the same thing about me in her journal). She has called me fairly frequently, alarmed by what she knows of my conversations with Arkeem.

Bert said she talked to a "discreet source in the D.A.'s office" about my revenge threats to try to figure out what she should do. It was for my own good, she said. It's over with Bert. I simply cannot trust her anymore. She really fucked up and has harmed me immeasurably because of her white, middle-class naïveté. She was first and foremost seeking to shield herself from liability, preserve her own career. What the hell does she think a D.A. is? Doesn't she know they're just cops in suits and could arrest me? I'm lost.

It's fifteen minutes past midnight. I've stopped crying and my eyelids feel fat. I cried from the heart, trying to wash out all my sadness. I wanted Daddy to come back from death and sit with me. I asked him to come but he didn't answer. Just as well. I would've been frightened. Bert called tonight after ten. It's so wrenching to talk to her. I think that's why I cried so much. I have no one else to talk to but Bert. She said if I do what I've threatened it will be catastrophic and that I want to punish her. I don't think so. I love Bert. She said if I stick with her I will be able to get some peace without having to kill. Is that true? I'm afraid to let myself be drawn back to her—she is so powerful. Again, I'll choose to live, convinced by her that the pain will end, only to be crushed by something new. I trust her but the force and impetus of my hatred and fear of *him* is overwhelming. He'll always find new ways to hurt me. I can't live with that, with him in this world.

I guess I understand more why Bert had to talk to someone in the D.A.'s office. As she put it, she would be "canned" otherwise. She said she also wanted to intimidate me out of acting on my fantasies.

Shit!!! Arkeem's been caught. Mother just told me. This is the end. The cops were waiting for him outside Jean's place. They threatened to charge her with harboring a fugitive if he didn't cooperate, so he did. The uneasy hope I had that Arkeem would take care of things for me is receding, shriveling up. What happens now? Do I dare act alone? Somewhere out there is a psychopath who wants to harm me. Doing nothing means a slow death, killing him first means an even slower death in prison.

It's on-campus recruiting season. I had an interview with Maximilian von Steen, a partner at Worthing & Schuster. I hope I get the offer. Everyone says Underwood & Hansen is a second-tier operation and not a major firm. Worthing & Schuster is twice the size, genteel and refined—their blood runs blue. I'd accept if they offered.

I had a nightmare I was raped in a closet by a big, fat, white detective.

He's back behind bars! I'm saved—and safe. Zimmerman just told me! He enjoyed his early release and stolen freedom just long enough to file a multimillion dollar lawsuit and hurt a few more people. It was all so predictable and so unnecessary. The courts should never have let loose a career rapist in the first place to prey on more women.

Worthing & Schuster made me an offer! I'm so happy I've been riding my skateboard back and forth in the apartment. Mother's pleased, too, and started "joking" about buying new linoleum and a living-room couch with the "allowance" I'm going to give her.

I now have two offers to choose from but I already know my choice—definitely Worthing & Schuster. They have gorgeous offices overlooking Rockefeller Center. When it rains it pours good news—after working feverishly I completed my article on the Fourth Amendment, footnotes and all, and submitted it to the journal for publication approval and staff edit. I'm thoroughly proud of myself. My next goal is to pass all my exams.

Thursday, I met Zimmerman for the first time, in the State Attorney's Office in the World Trade Center. Very straight, square, solid man. Not tall. Looks over the top of his glasses when he talks. Nice. He appeared embarrassed and nervous but seemed sincere and honest. He said the trial will probably be held in a year and will essentially be a full-scale rape trial, even though it's ostensibly civil. It will be "bloody" and they'll use everything they have to attack my sanity, credibility, and truthfulness. We talked for two hours in a small room. I felt like a scared child. I asked the fundamental question—do I *have* to testify? He said he can't force me to take part since I'm only a "third-party witness" and that it's my decision. Apparently, the rapist was involved in a number of "similar incidents" while he was out, always using the same m.o. The trial will be before "an abrasive and brilliant arch-conservative judge who's a reformed alcoholic and devout Catholic."

I've been sleeping fitfully and am always on edge. I have to put this daytime nightmare out of my mind and focus on the hurdle ahead—passing the bar exam. Yesterday was the first day of my bar-review course. Felt psyched. I can pass if I can block out everything else.

I can't wait to graduate and begin my career. I'll have a job, money, an apartment. My life will be mine. I'm full of shrapnel but determined to survive.

Bert and I talked today for the last time. She said she would keep seeing me if she could, but can't. I can't keep enrolling at Columbia—the Health Service won't have it anymore. Flunked Bengali anyway. It's killing me. Two nights ago, I dreamed I was hanging by my hands on to a rock, a rocky terrain gaping beneath me. Two women were sitting atop the rocks, one of whom I recognized from *Law Review*. I was afraid to fall and held on desperately, trying to seem unruffled as I dangled. "Can you help me get up?" I asked. The one I knew said, "Just move your hand to that rock." I did, and fell. I woke up midway my fall, upset.

Bar exam—sometimes I think I might, most times I'm afraid I can't. Pass, that is. I'm pushing though. Physically, I'm developing the stamina to study from 7 a.m. to midnight daily without too much pain.

Exams are over. How does it feel to be done with law school? I don't know. For the past month, all I feel is anger and all I do is fantasize about death.

Nineteen more days before the bar exam. I miss Bert and cry when I think about how she saved my life.

Two more days! I'm nervous but I should pass.

The bar exam is over. I'm frazzled. Not sure I passed. It's possible I didn't. The multiple-choice questions were difficult and I was unsure of many (most) of my answers. I did well on only two out of the six essays. Nerves. Fright. Angst.

I signed a lease yesterday for an apartment in a luxury high-rise building a block from Central Park, with a twenty-four-hour doorman, a health club on the fiftieth floor, camera surveillance in the lobby, and no fucking rapist bastards. It's a high-class fortress and I'll be safe. It even has a *name*: The Sheffield. My thirtieth-floor studio has a spectacular view of Manhattan and the river. From projects to plush.

One of my recurrent fantasies has come true. Yesterday, the journal held its third annual alumni affair. Late, I stuck on my name tag and slipped very quietly into Greenberg Lounge. A friend rushed up and kissed me. "Congratulations! You were just named for the Best Student Note award!" "Get out of here," I said, laughing, not believing a word of it. He gestured to a journal colleague standing at the podium. "Here's Janet McDonald," she said into a microphone. Everyone looked my way, applauding. All my friends, some proud, some pretending, were all clapping for *me*. Even Dean Redlich. It was unreal. I'm going to receive $100 at graduation and be officially recognized at the ceremony! The perfect culmination of my NYU ordeal. I often dreamed of getting some kind of award at graduation, of coming full circle. I'm so excited I could scream. I'm famous! Beloved! A legend! Dean Redlich came over and congratulated me. "Thank you," I said, genuinely moved, "and thank you for taking me back." Minutes later he called me away from a crowd of admiring friends to say he would be willing to submit an affidavit on my behalf to the character committee of the bar. White men: they make you, they break you. A few years ago he's calling for me to be locked up for twenty-five years, now he is willing to throw around the power and prestige of his White Maleness to make it all better. Hey, I'll take it.

The bar results are out. My two study partners failed. Darlene, the most confident of our group, said she failed because of the multiple-choice questions. I'm not surprised Jackie failed, though. Every time I called her up to ask a question, she was watching the soaps. Studying made her too nervous, she said. I probably failed, too.

I passed!

I passed!

I passed!

Yes, I passed, but I still woke up and cried first thing this morning. Unfortunately, life doesn't end with passing the bar exam. I wish it did. Same ol' me, same ol' sadness. Life continues.

Graduation was wonderful. Mother, Paulette, Kevin, and all four nieces went—in a 1956 Rolls-Royce. A white, uniformed chauffeur who seemed genuinely pleased to participate in the fantasy of a project family. It was pure melodrama and ostentation, done in fun. We cruised through the projects and people gaped. They gaped in Manhattan as we rolled down Fifth Avenue, Kevin hanging out one window screaming "I just won Lotto!" Makeeba hanging out another yelling, "I'm Whitney Houston's cousin!" and the rest of us laughing wildly. The ceremony was held in the Jacob Javits Convention Center. When the Dean of Students announced the winner of the award for the best student-written article—Janet McDonald—I floated down the aisle and across the stage like Miss Universe to accept my award certificate and hundred-dollar check. The audience applauded. The McDonalds broke with decorum, of course, and shouted, "Go, Janet!" while making barking sounds. Mother and Paulette were in tears. At thirty-two, years after my Cornell classmates, I became a law-school graduate. As rowdily as possible we piled into our Rolls and were driven back to Brooklyn.

I walked by Kim Yoo on Fifty-seventh Street today. She was on the arm of another Lennonesque whiteboy. She looked over her shoulder at me at the same moment I looked back at her. We kept walking.

PART

3

My legal career at Worthing & Schuster began in midtown Manhattan amid broad smiles and rough handshakes. In the hierarchical world of corporate law firms, the first job on one's résumé can be a determinative career move; I had the "right" name on mine. I was introduced to a gauntlet of hotshot lawyers whose names I couldn't remember and taken to lunch at an expensive restaurant. The recruiting committee's luncheon group included an associate who had been a student at NYU at the time of the fires. Watching me intently, he said, "Your name sounds so familiar . . ." I mumbled something about the commonness of ordinary names. I was so petrified he'd realize who I was that most of my lunch was left uneaten.

Gradually, I settled into a yuppie routine. I lived in a fifty-story, high-rent, high-rise apartment building that overlooked the Hudson River and enjoyed walking down Fifth Avenue every morning to my office. The outfit I wore was so similar to everyone else's that we resembled marchers in a parade. It rarely varied from a black Burberry's all-weather trench coat, a Jones New York suit with white cotton tailored blouse, and black leather low-heeled Gucci shoes. The walk was what I liked most about my workday. That, and the late-night taxi ride home. I took pleasure not so much in the comfortable ride but in the sound of the cab braking to stop. What a change from the squeal of tires swerving to pass me by in favor of the nearest white traveler, or the rumble of acceleration as a cab hailed by a white decoy friend sped away when I approached. Before moving to Manhattan, I couldn't even *bribe* a cabbie of *any race* to take me home. "I don't go to Brooklyn," was the standard refrain. They all did, of course, but to Brooklyn Heights, or Cobble Hill or Park Slope, not to the projects. My new look got the cabs to stop, and three magic words transported me home. "The Sheffield, please." "On Fifty-seventh? No problem."

The two places I called "home" were markers at very extreme poles of my life. The projects were rich with the ruins of my personal history. The odor of tight elevators, the echo of narrow stairwells, the crunch of the gravel-covered roof, such things erased my present and held me to the past. I no longer belonged *in* the projects, but still *to* them. And when I was there, the place did the remembering, not me. It whispered memories about my struggles and hopes, failures and violence. Manhattan was also home. Defying my project-girl destiny had landed me in a lobby of wall-length mirrors and gaudy chandeliers, mingling with models, rock musicians, a former congressman, black women in furs, and other well-heeled Manhattanites. They came and went with ease and deferential greetings from the uniformed doormen. My routine greeting was, "Miss! Can I help you?" and it made little difference how often I was introduced by the concierge as a tenant. The Sheffield blotted out my past with its nouveau riche dazzle, and negated my present by its outright denial of my existence. In the projects, I was a ghost, and in my high-rise, invisible. At first I felt apologetic, as though I was doing something wrong simply by being there. I *didn't* belong. Which was precisely why I wanted to be there. I loved standing out unpleasantly, a raindrop on the parade of the rich and famous, representing the dreaded black underclass of drug-addicted, neighbor-mugging monsters. The Sheffield was a fortress against people like me: I relished being the one who had moved in right next door. I furnished my studio à la Early Prison Cell with a platform bed, bookcase, television, cassette player, desk and chair. I wrote in my journal: "I look out over the river, watch people sunbathing on rooftops, and take in the sunset, moonrise, sky, wind, and quiet, all in total safety." I was even excited about receiving my first phone bill.

After shelling out thousand-dollar monthly rent payments along with everyone else, I began to feel entitled to a little respect. As a corporate lawyer project girl with degrees from three of the country's top schools, I was not about to accept being dissed by door-men. So when they would ask if they could "help" me, I'd snap, "No. I *live* here, remember?" and keep walking. Eventually, they got it. "Oh! Miss McDonald. Sorry. Have a nice day." The irony of my one-woman campaign was that, in truth, there was little that seemed genuinely project about me by the time I moved into the Sheffield. But the projects had formed me. I knew in my gut what it felt like to risk your life simply by taking the stairs or getting on the wrong side of a cop's mood. And that awareness kept me close to my origins.

Most of my neighbors were true to type and looked through me when we encountered one another in the building's common areas. Which made the sudden appearance of Sally at my door all the more surprising. "I saw you moving in and thought I'd drop by and welcome you to the Sheffield. I'm two doors down. Why don't you come by for a drink?" I was so nonplussed by her age, accent, and friendliness that I agreed, even though I rarely drank. Sipping a Scotch on the rocks, Sally talked about her deceased husbands and her life as an artist. She showed me some of her paintings and said she'd invented and patented a kind of carbon-copy paper used by artists. I'd grown to like Southern accents and delighted in hers. An aging poodle she called Baby shared the spacious apartment with Sally, who was eighty-one years old. She looked much younger than her years and I told her so. In her lush twang she said, "Well, I should hope so. I've had five face-lifts!" I visited often and she never answered the door empty-handed. Her arrival was routinely announced by the familiar clink of ice cubes in her omnipresent Scotch. We were an unlikely pair but well suited to each other's needs. Sally was obviously lonely and I enjoyed having at least one friend in the Sheffield.

Between the morning walk to the office and the night ride to my high-rise home lay the job. Worthing & Schuster was typical of the behemoth law firms that consumed hordes of fresh law grads culled from all across the country. I sought, in vain, to find a place in the firm's well-entrenched caste system. The partnership was overwhelmingly white and male, and the mail room completely black and male. A small number of lawyers, and most of the secretaries, were white women. The firm's "feeder" undergrad and law schools provided enough ivy to choke on, with Columbia, Wellesley, Harvard, Vassar, and Yale being the most widely represented. The club was so mercilessly exclusive that even short people had it bad—no partner, including the one woman partner, was less than six feet tall. "Today I left my office and walked to the elevator bank, where I stood alone. Over the dark brown heavy door, in gold lettering, I read Worthing & Schuster and felt proud and honored that they would have me, and eager to make good," I wrote in my journal. I also had other, more pointed feelings.

My colleagues were from the middle and upper classes, and as much as I tried, I could not quiet an inner rumbling of hostility.

"I feel a degree of contempt for the shallowness, subconscious racism, and naïveté of my spoiled colleagues." One evening, walking in Greenwich Village with associates from work, I greeted a friend who clearly was living in the streets. "You know him?!" shrieked one of my colleagues. I was angered that they *didn't* know him, and in fact would *never* know anyone in his predicament.

I had finally made it inside the club doors, yet felt more like an outsider than ever. Acutely aware of my nonentity status—nonwhite, non-male, and non-upper class—I went ahead and erased myself completely. I buried my project girl and told co-workers I was originally from Brooklyn Heights. Project Girl wasn't the only fatality; I also killed off several siblings, leaving a more appropriately sized, two-kid family. And what does your brother do? they asked. "Oh, Kevin? He's in college at Vassar, following in my footsteps."

The other two black lawyers shied away from me and each other. The rationale went, and probably still goes, like this: if "they" saw "us" hanging out together, it meant you were not a team player, not client-friendly, and thus not partnership material, meaning you had no future at the firm. I would have liked to share my experiences with another black Worthing & Schuster lawyer but it wasn't going to happen. I continued making the big and little compromises, wearing the pinstripes and the pumps, isolated and worn down. I worked the long hours, ate expensive sushi lunches, and prattled on about my year in Europe. Bert had been right—there was nothing but a crater at the top of the mountain. And inside that crater were jarring reminders of who I really was.

On my way to the office one morning, I made a stop at the cash machine on the corner of Fifty-seventh Street and Eighth Avenue. Through the glass door of the bank I saw a black man seated on a ledge, hurriedly scribbling in a drawing pad. He was trying to sketch people in the few minutes it takes to do a bank-machine transaction, in hopes of selling the "portraits." Young professionals dressed like me waited in line at cash dispensers. They glanced warily at the artist-in-residence. No one even looked up in response to his "Uh, scuse me." In fact, people recoiled. I knew they were afraid, because I was, too. I debated whether to go to a different banking outlet but decided to take my chances.

Like the others, I approached the cash machine without looking at him but was aware of his every move. I was relieved to get my money and quickly turned to leave. Our eyes met. "*McDonald!* You Butter's sister! Damn! Come here and gimme a hug! How you doin'?!" It had been ages since I had heard Ernest's teenage nickname, Butter, a tag he got for his love of Butternut candy bars. "David Junior! Hi! I didn't . . . um . . . realize that was you. How're *you* doing?" We hugged and stepped outside onto Fifty-seventh Street. Bank customers continued to stream by, shutting us both out of their awareness. "Girl, I'm fucked up! You see what I'm doing, right?! I just got out the joint. Homeless and shit. Man, they fucked me up in jail. Lost my eye, see? If you could help me out . . ." The momentary happiness inspired by this unexpected encounter with home vanished. I recalled D.J. strutting around the projects, joking, flirting, getting in trouble, shooting hoops in the park with other boys. I reached in my coat pocket, pulled out a bill I didn't bother to look at, and handed it to him. "Ten? Nah, I can't take that," he protested, his hand reaching for the bill. "It's so good to see you," he said, pushing the bill in his pocket. Then he asked the question I dreaded. "You out the projects, right? So, where you live now?" "Upstairs." "You live here?!" he shouted, leaning far back to take in the full fifty stories of the Sheffield. He cracked up laughing and hugged me again. "Damn, girl! You doin' *real* good." I said I really had to get to work. "Thanks, McDonald. Yo, tell Butter I'm gonna come by one of these days and shoot some hoops with him. Your mom's doing all right? Tell her I said hello. Uh, listen, you got a phone number?" I smiled and shook my head. He smiled, too, as though he understood. Of course not. David Junior went back to his seat inside the bank and set the sketch pad on his lap, still smiling. I walked glumly to work.

Head-on collisions with my past weren't always with project people. There was the time when I was waiting for the shuttle train at Times Square and happened to look up from my newspaper right into Lou Tribe's face. I stared. Hallucination? Dream? Silently, I mouthed, "Lou?" He said, "Janet! I thought that was you!" It had been seventeen years since I'd seen my revolutionary hero from Erasmus. The only news I'd heard was a rumor that he'd become paranoid about being pursued by the FBI and had barricaded himself in his brother's upstate house for a long time. Over the years, I'd never stopped thinking about the boy who could've been Sal Mineo's twin. Reality contrasted sharply with that memory. I confided my new impressions to my journal: "Lou was heavier, unshaven, grungy, and scruffy-looking. I was afraid to ask him what he was doing because I thought he might be homeless. In dreams and memory he was always bigger than life. This morning at 9 a.m. on the subway platform he looked quite smaller than life, and felt injured to me, somehow broken or hurt (maybe it was the post-nervous-breakdown look in his eyes)." I felt that *he* was impressed by *me*. "Lawyer?" He laughed. "I thought you were a law-*breaker*! I guess you had us all fooled." He wanted to know what kind of law I practiced and I mumbled "corporate." "Wow, Janet!" We both chuckled. "More power to you," he said. I was relieved he didn't condemn me for growing up to be a military-industrial-complex flunky. We talked about friends from high school and *The Midnight Rambler*. I mentioned the green army bag he carried that said: "I Am Waiting for a Rebirth of Wonder." "I still am," he said, laughing. We exchanged business cards, promising to stay in touch. His bore an address in the East Village and read "Photographer. Certificate in Psychotherapy." My last journal comment was, "It was thrilling, yet anticlimactic. He doesn't look like Sal Mineo, after all. Maybe Judy Kroll isn't mythic either. Or Bert." We never did get in touch.

My life in the unforgiving world of the private law firm was debilitating. Months of journal entries recount feelings of loneliness, incompetence, and awkwardness. Work is "terrible" and "boring," punctuated by the all too frequent "nightmare luncheon." I was routinely working from early morning until late at night and described a typical day: "I worked from 8 a.m. to 9 p.m., researching pension plans and the legislative history of sections of the Internal Revenue Code, came home after a lonesome dinner at Hatsuhana, and fell on the bed crying." Another entry talks of working three consecutive days until past midnight on a bond deal. Another relates a "four-day nightmare": "At trial-advocacy training Lisa forgot her closing argument and I got yelled at for doing a wimpy cross-examination. 'You would've been dead in the water!' shouted Kearney, star litigator. But at the mock awards ceremony I still got a tiny plastic trophy for tearing apart the witness—a shrink—on cross-examination. How appropriate. I feel uncomfortable socializing with the white men. Silence and smiles prevail, but no conversation."

This minor victory was immediately overshadowed by the deadening pace of work. For weeks at a time, I worked feverishly until 11 p.m., hounded by partners coming at me from all directions. "You need a lesson in letter writing. Don't say 'Please find enclosed,' say 'I enclose.' " "Would you like to try your hand at drafting these corporate resolutions?" "We gotta get this stuff out *today*." "I need the draft we did *after* the one we sent to Saipan, not this one." "Did you talk to Peter?" "Did you talk to Mike Welsh?" "Call Farlon Stevens." "Your secretary's looking for you —I'm looking for you, too." Underlying all my frenetic work activity was a marked reserve to the whole process. Often, I felt as though I was going through the motions, not fully applying myself, but doing only enough to get by. However, doing even a "get-by" level of work at such a firm required Herculean effort.

The psychic forces driving my self-sabotaging behavior were complex and obscure to me. In part, success filled me with a sense of guilt that probably stemmed from my resented school successes as a child. I feared the jealousy and envy of others. But that wasn't my only fear. I was also afraid of failing to be number one. My self-esteem had been built on a foundation of certificates of excellence, merit awards, and special recognitions of all sorts. But basic boredom and hostility to the work I was doing made it impossible for me to summon the energy necessary to shine. And if I couldn't be a socially approved star, I'd be its shadow counterpart, a rebel. I mastered the art of smoke and mirrors: appearing to be in the office using a jacket casually left as a prop on a chair back, when I was actually at the gym; repeatedly dashing off to the bar-association library, so conveniently located near the Times Square movie theaters; reading a novel held inside some dull treatise propped up on my desk.

I had mundane issues to grapple with as well, such as learning to play boss to a secretary. My secretary, who was black, described herself as a "centered Buddhist," which made it all the more puzzling why she could not transcend stress long enough to produce a typo-free document. I shared Jackie with two colleagues, young, white guys who had no problem getting used to bossing and criticizing. The three of us would meet regularly in one of our offices to discuss the "Jackie problem." As a secretary, Jackie was quite exasperating, but she was nice and I was touched by her pride in the firm's only black female associate—me. My male colleagues were not encumbered by such sentiments. They wanted me to join them in giving her a negative performance evaluation. A lawyer's critical evaluation automatically meant no annual raise and sometimes led to probation. Just like a white boy, I thought, to want to fuck with somebody's money. I refused. Instead, I warned Jackie she had to improve. She made all the right promises, then handed me a memo I had drafted for Maximilian von Steen, the partner who had interviewed me at NYU and brought me to the firm. In that relaxed school setting, I had no idea he was an anal-compulsive who found errors with the accuracy of a heat-seeking missile. Seconds into his minute examination of page one, he found a typo. "This is unacceptable, Janet. Our clients demand perfection and that's what the firm asks of associates." I returned to my office feeling defeated, wanting to be angry with Jackie, but unable to be. On one hand, I suffered because of the poor work she did for me, but on the other I thought, so what if she makes mistakes—so do I. I was unable to resolve my conflict because I identified too strongly with the young black woman struggling to succeed in an unwelcoming corporate world ruled by white males.

I now looked forward to weekends in the projects. There, my mere existence meant success, and I had nothing to prove. I hung out in front of the building, practiced new dances, memorized current slang, and got caught up on neighborhood news. Ann had moved back home to Mother's apartment; Jean was still living downstairs. Each had two daughters, a second generation of project girls. Ann's life continued to revolve around drugs, despite the deaths of scores of friends and intimates. Jean worked as a secretary and enrolled her daughters in private schools she could barely afford, desperate to preserve them from "project life." My nieces were smart and energetic. One wrote poems about Martin Luther King, Jr., another mastered computers, all of them "college material." The boys had ventured farther away from home, except for Kevin, who worked odd jobs and still lived with Mother. Victor was stationed in Germany. Ernest was drug-free and stayed out of trouble, but his criminal record seemed always to sabotage job prospects. He was receiving public assistance and raising two boys in another Brooklyn neighborhood. Luke had settled down in San Francisco with his partner and sometimes worked as a movie extra.

We had all stumbled. Most of us had gotten back up, others not quite.

I was the only child in a financial position to help the family, and I did so with flair, doling out money like a philanthropist. My father's death had left Mother dependent on small social-security payments, her sole source of income. I supplemented it as I could. It was a pleasure to take the whole family to Broadway shows, Dance Theater of Harlem performances, Vassar Club dinners, and other places they could never go. They would descend on Manhattan like tourists in a foreign country, posing and snapping photos. I no longer had any illusions about inspiring anyone to follow in my footsteps with such outings. I simply enjoyed sharing my new world with them. Along with "allowances," I gave gifts, bought clothes, and paid for dental care. On holidays, I hand-delivered my own flowers and fruit baskets because a spate of robberies had caused merchants to refuse to deliver to the projects. Along with the family subsidies, I had my own rent, expenses, and debts to pay. The corporate world's "golden handcuffs" I'd been warned about in law school were tightening around my wrists.

My old neighbors in Farragut took vicarious pride in my doings. It wasn't that other project kids hadn't also found their own paths to productive lives. Some had finished high school and found jobs commensurate with their education, a couple had graduated college and become schoolteachers, a few had completed health-care aide-training programs. One particularly remarkable family had produced not only a teacher and a lawyer but a professional basketball player and a male model as well. What distinguished me from those other success stories, however, was very simple—visibility. My accomplished peers were rarely seen in the projects. I don't judge their absence, as I am sure there were undoubtedly many reasons for it: parents move away, careers require relocating to distant places, new families are started elsewhere. Whatever the explanation, the fact remained that they were not often seen around the neighborhood or at the annual "Farragut Day." As for me, I felt lost if I didn't go home periodically. That presence kept my own achievement very real to others. "You a lawyer? I knew you was gonna make it. The Man can't keep *all* of us down. You keep on keeping on, sister." Then came the inevitable solicitation. "Check this out, I got busted, right, for this stickup I didn't do. Now the D.A.'s saying if I cop this plea, I'm out in three to five, but if I go to trial . . ." I would politely interrupt and chuckle at the inevitable response, *"Business?!"* Parents of childhood class-mates would say, beaming, "Haven't seen you in ages, Miss Law-yer." At those moments, I felt I was giving them something, even if it was merely symbolic. My success was theirs as well. I was one of their own who had "made good," and not disappeared. It was only at work that I felt like an abject failure.

It seemed symbolic that I was doing bond work. I felt as if I were *in* bondage as my life slipped out from beneath my feet; it no longer belonged to me but to the firm. The exhaustion and dis-satisfaction I felt robbed my efforts of meaning. I asked myself why I was doing it. "Where am I going and why? So that on the two days I have to myself I can afford to live in a luxurious yuppie sty?" So that was it? Making it, moving on up, becoming a yuppie, buppie, bourgeois, or whatever meant looking like a nun in black coat and black shoes, feeling empty with a walletful of money? My stressful experience wasn't unusual for beginner lawyers. What made it particularly unwieldy for me, however, was the sharp clash between this new world and what I still thought of as my *real* world.

En route to NYU to do some research, I ran into an old friend in Washington Square Park. I had fond memories of Bucky but hadn't seen him for years. As a boy he had been what we girls called "fly," a good-looking kid with dark, laughing eyes. I remem-bered him stepping and sliding in rhythm with his friends, as the lead singer of a roughneck version of the Temptations, harmonizing in the lobby of my mother's building. Unlike most of the boys I grew up with, Bucky had succeeded in avoiding both jail and the snare of drugs. As we grew older, he was always curious about my schooling. "You *still* in school?!" he'd gasp, feigning, or maybe not, shock. I always enjoyed our talks. But that day on the bench I struggled for something to say. Bucky had "bugged," and it was obvious. He said he was in a men's shelter, "just temporarily," until he got himself together. His sooty and disheveled appearance belied the qualification. As we talked, his eyes darted from one place to another, and his halting conversation gave voice to a stream of confused and broken thoughts.

Seated in front of a stack of Internal Revenue Code treatises, I found it impossible to concentrate. It troubled me that so many friends from the neighborhood were not making it intact out of their twenties and thirties. Their faces surged from memory, eyes holding plans and hopes for futures that we didn't know were already closed off—a priori, as the lawyers said. The ties I felt were sometimes strained to the snapping point. I was sickened by the newspaper accounts of exactly how many times my close friend Ellen stabbed our neighbor when he refused to give her crack money. But I also knew that her life had been derailed when she gave birth at age fourteen to a baby fathered by an adult neighbor. I cringed for my twenty-something project girlfriends trumpeted in newspaper headlines as the Bankrobber Girl Gang. Filmed by bank surveillance cameras placing high-caliber withdrawal slips in front of startled tellers, they were all sent to prison. I remembered the young black twenty-something hit man promoting his services with the offer, "I usually get two grand to off somebody, but I'll kill any nigger for five dollars," and Mother's description of the neighborhood AIDS epidemic: "Nobody's getting shot that much anymore—now they just laying down dying." I thought back to the day Ann came by my job to "borrow" twenty dollars. The receptionist's words were normal, but her voice betrayed disdain.

"Miss McDonald, you have a visitor in reception." I rushed out and hurried Ann to my office. Her skinny body barely filled the dingy sweat-suit outfit she wore, and her sunken eyes and gray skin said what anyone with eyes could see: she was a junkie. She had been that way for so long that I couldn't remember her ever looking any different. I gave her the money, slipped her out the firm's back door, and cried in my office for a long time. Such thoughts and memories soured any satisfaction I might take in my own success.

Work was grinding me down, and not only the hours. I was not invited to client meetings like my white male counterparts, nor did I have a mentor ready to champion my cause if ever I came up for partner. I looked forward to the firm's annual "retreat" and hoped that in a more sociable context I would be able to bond with a possible mentor. The mentoring process provided for a more focused connection between powerful partners and ambitious associates and was an essential part of associate training and grooming.

The selection of the Sleepy Hollow Country Club for our retreat, where one of the partners belonged, sparked controversy because of its rumored policy forbidding black and Jewish members. I was excited to be going to yet another place where I wasn't wanted. The day was magnificent, with deep greens and lush blues. At the country club, I cynically played WASP, taking golf lessons and smoking an awful cigar at dinner with our cigar-smoking partner. I played tennis and Frisbee and danced cheek-to-cheek with a Clark Kent look-alike "to some horrible jitterbug music played by a band of four old, dreary men," as I wrote. All my white male WASP bonding efforts failed. Not only did I leave the club without a mentor; I also left without my sneakers.

That's when the true fun began. The only person I knew in New York who owned a car was Paulette, my Brooklyn buddy. As hostile to the upper classes as I, she readily agreed to drive me back to the "rich bastards' club," as she put it, where our kind was not welcome. The day after the firm retreat, Paulette and I returned to stares and haughty airs. Thoroughly pleased, I strolled over to the "Members Only" reception desk. "Hi! I was here yesterday with Worthing & Schuster and forgot my sneakers in the locker room," I announced brightly. The desk attendant directed us to the "Ladies' Lounge." No one had stolen them. Then I assessed the unique opportunity we had. "Paulette, let's steal a golf cart and ride around. No one will stop us—you just sit back and look like a rich blond bitch, and I'll be your black caddy. It's perfect." She protested that it was a crazy idea, but in the end she couldn't resist either. I sped all over the grounds, Paulette next to me roaring, "You're going too fast! We're gonna tip over!" A couple of times we stopped to take in the breathtaking views of distant sailboats and estates. Then we'd speed around the green again. I had much more fun than the previous day, and no one questioned us, so appropriate did we look.

When the time came to assign associates to departments, I stated my interest in international law. Yet I was relegated to the employment-law department, where my black femaleness would be useful in defending corporate clients charged with race or sex discrimination. Jackie was put on probation and eventually let go, leaving me with no real ally. Occasional collisions took place between my muffled resentment and certain partners' blaring egos. More experienced associates consoled me with explanations about men on power trips, men who liked to abuse and intimidate, men who were divorced and still angry at women. Shrug it off, they said. I wrote bitterly about working fifteen hours a day for a month with a certain Henry C.: "His sixty-year-old white colleagues chuckle at my complaints and say, 'Yes, Henry can be a bit crusty.' I am a first-year associate, nervous, insecure, black, female, and frightened . . . All I experience is a tall, irascible, nasty bastard who demoralizes me by snidely criticizing everything I do and who grimaces and winces when I ask questions. I've been on the verge of tears for three days." Behind the tears, a volcano of anger was building, triggered by what felt like abusive rather than crusty behavior. Its source, however, was fueled by upheaval unrelated to work stress.

"The woman from Victim's Services talked to me for about a half hour about the upcoming trial and was very supportive," I wrote about the civil trial, which continued to hang over me like Damocles' sword. "I don't have much fight left in me. I'm in so much pain, sometimes acute, sometimes dull, but always constant. I cry in stores and at work, hiding the tears. Everything is throbbing and aching in me as I go through each day mortally wounded. I don't even ask 'Why me?' anymore. Now it just feels like, 'Yes, me.' All I can do is tell the truth about what happened. But the truth is weak. Lying prevails in our legal system and he lies well." Bert was unavailable to me, since she didn't have a private practice, and I could no longer use Columbia's mental-health facilities, which were reserved for students. At the time, I couldn't see how profoundly I was being affected by the case. So much was new in my life—the job, the apartment, my altered relationship with my family and with myself—that I missed the forest for the trees. I thought it was just one more thing. In fact, it was the only thing. There was no undertow greater than the threat of the civil trial and what it potentially could do to my life. The worst aspect of it was that I found myself in a lose-lose situation. If I didn't testify, the State would lose and have to pay, and if I did testify . . . it was too awful to contemplate. Friends told me to be courageous and hold on to my dignity. All I could come up with for myself were project-girl fantasies about a dramatic courtroom revenge shooting.

The stress was unbearable. And since I couldn't bear it, I shut my emotions off so I wouldn't feel it. The effect was like putting a top on a whistling teapot. "Friday, I stormed out of work at two in the afternoon, angry and crying because dickbrain Vincent, the employment-law partner, was being his usual self, an asshole, just like that pig, Henry. All week, he'd been screaming and snapping at me. 'Janet, you're not a summer associate. I don't understand the problem you're having comprehending this.' There he stood before me, short and squat, stuffed in a blue suit, a remarried divorcé cheating on his second wife with a young airhead secretary who wants to be an actress. Something goes wrong, he's happy to pass the blame on to me; something goes right, he's even happier to take the credit. My head pounded as I responded politely, 'I see what you mean.' 'Now, I'll be back at six and I need the answer.' " I wasn't there at six and didn't care. Abusive partners, cheating husbands, lying rapists, all became one to me. And I was their victim. I reacted like trapped prey, nothing left but an animal's instinct to survive. I lashed out at my tormentors and took a leave of absence.

Shortly into my leave, I started making the headhunter rounds. One of them suggested I look for a position outside New York. She gushed about my "marketability." "With your credentials," she enthused, "you can write your own ticket." Another hunter, a black friend from law school, tried to persuade me to accept a law job in Tokyo I had been offered. "Imagine it, Janet, a black woman lawyer in Tokyo!" She downplayed the sixteen-hour days I would have to work, and the Japanese reputation for xenophobia and sexism. "Who cares?! You stay there two or three years, make a lot of money, and when you come back to New York you'll be a golden girl." A midsized, sixty-person Seattle firm wanted to interview me. Friends cautioned me against leaving the New York market, warning that I would be a big fish in a small pond, that I would have no mobility if ever I wanted to leave Seattle.

I no longer cared about ponds and golden girls. I wanted a little happiness and had begun to rethink my willingness, shared by most law-school graduates, to do anything that would "look good" on a résumé. Up to that point in my life, I had bought the whole illusion: go to the right schools, work at the right firm, live in the right neighborhood in the right city. All those "right" moves had proved to be dead wrong for me, and I wanted change. I imagined re-creating myself in a new environment. I wanted relief from my problems. Maybe the New York rat race made me crazy with competing to be the best, to be number one. Perhaps it was the family; if I went somewhere far away, I could focus on saving myself and not them. Or it might simply have been too complicated to be a young black college-educated woman from the projects. Whatever strain I felt from any of those causes was greatly magnified by the trial I so dreaded.

My role as family savior was wearing. I had grown tired of paying my siblings' constantly overdue rent, dental bills, and miscellaneous expenses, and sick of keeping everyone in the latest absurd fashions of gold chains, gold slip-on teeth, and expensive sneakers. Ann called so regularly to borrow money she never repaid that I began answering the phone with, "I don't have any money." I needed to be somewhere neutral where I could view my life from a fresh perspective, and New York just wasn't the place. I would interview for the job in Seattle. Mother had grown used to my wanderlust, beginning with my year in Paris and subsequent trips there. But she was still not pleased with my plans. "You sure want to get away from us, don't you? I looked on the map. Seattle is about as far away as you can go, without going straight into the ocean." I laughed. She was right, I *did* want to get away from the life I had in New York. I boarded a plane for Seattle, not quite sure what to expect from a city rated by a national magazine as "the most livable" in the United States.

My two interviewers were clean-cut-looking thirty-something

white men who were unable to hide their surprise that my résumé had led them to expect a white woman. I presented myself wrapped in the shiny allure of "New York lawyer," and armed with clichés about New York's "cutthroat" law practices and Seattle's "human values," I got the job offer. Somehow, the easy willingness of these Seattlelites to hire me seemed in character with the kind of people who would battle to save a spotted owl. I felt I was endangered, too, and hoped to be saved.

At the very beginning of August, Mother and I stood outside the building, watching a friend load my suitcases into his car. "Today?" she asked softly. "You didn't tell me you were leaving for Seattle today." I felt awful. I thought I had given her my exact departure date, but maybe I hadn't. So much was always left unsaid between us. "Yes, I did," I said, forcing a guilty smile. Sorrow billowed inside me. I was leaving home without a return ticket for the first time, going as far away as I could go before hitting the ocean. New York life was just too rugged, too unforgiving. "Oh, it's only a six-hour flight," I said, falsely dismissive. The car was packed and the driver ready. "Well, I gotta see a man about a horse," I said, averting my eyes from hers. We embraced, exchanged truncated "love you"s, and I left the projects.

Seattle air smelled clean and the city felt small and manageable. I moved in August to a four-story housing complex and was instantly duped by the weather. "Up to this point, the weather has been stunning, a blue sky full of sunlight," I wrote. I shared the apartment with another non-native, a woman from Kalamazoo. "I didn't know that was a real place—I thought it was just a song," I told Annie, a soft-spoken former airline worker. She had amusing nicknames for airlines, like Northwest Scare and US Dare, was planning to enroll in school as a Black Studies major, and was fit as a bodybuilder. I noticed that most of the natives also looked extremely fit. At the firm, the men were often without ties and the women wore dresses and skirts instead of the obligatory pin-striped suit. What with the great company of my new roommate and the laid-back attitude of the other lawyers, I was thoroughly pleased with the move within two weeks of my arrival. "Seattle is vintage cars, massage therapy, and Asian restaurants. The people are nice, and *very* white, but the city is not racially tense and polarized like New York. There are women construction workers and everyone is shockingly trusting; Annie and I went to buy mountain bikes and the salesman let us do a test ride in a park a block away. Cars and doors are left unlocked and you can pay for things with checks."

The pacific environment of the Northwest provided a perfect backdrop for peace talks between my inner warring factions. Not surprisingly, the talks began with recriminations. "If you, Vassar Girl, hadn't adopted such white male values, life would've gone smoother." "Well, if you, Project Girl, hadn't been so concerned with proving you're not white, my life would have been much easier." With time, the hubbub quieted down and I began to accept all my selves. In freeing myself of my personal stereotypes, I was able to see others more clearly. The people I got to know wore human faces, not the masks I projected onto them. At Vassar, I was so locked in my private woes that I failed to see the misery of the unhappy, uncared-for rich kids I thought led such enviable lives. Seattle had its own version of the same group, but now I could recognize them. A fellow lawyer's casual trumpeting of her privileged background belied her torment over failing to measure up to the legacy of her prominent politican father. The son of a well-known New York diplomat had opted for a low-powered Seattle law practice to escape the burden of the name he bore like a cross. True friendship proved impossible with such class casualties, for whom my race and background were feathers in their politically correct caps, and the rest of me irrelevant. The positive aspect of such painful encounters was that I developed a new appreciation for my own background and family. I realized, to my surprise, that my life had given me a psychic and spiritual stamina that money, connections, and privilege could not offer.

Fortunately, most people I met in this largely middle-class city were down-to-earth and genuinely friendly. Early on, I became friends with Nancy Kennedy, a witty, smart, open-minded lawyer whose office was next to mine. Married to a lawyer and the mother of two daughters, she had all the trappings of the standard middle-class life-style. Yet we developed a solid friendship, formed no doubt from our healthy curiosity about each other. We had long talks about my life in the projects, her Irish Catholic upbringing in Ohio, the death penalty, race . . . no topic was too far afield for our lunchtime roundtables. Sometimes they didn't even occur at lunch. I wrote about her in my journal. "Yesterday I went into Nancy Kennedy's office at about 4:30 to see how she was doing. We started talking about God, good and evil, the book *When Bad Things Happen to Good People,* and her troubled brother, who came from their perfect white middle-class, Middle Western, caring family and still suffered. She believes that people are not evil, just screwed up. That's compassionate. I thought of the rapist . . . evil or screwed up? By the time we decided to get back to work, we looked at our watches and were shocked. It was almost 6 p.m.! We stared at each other and burst out laughing." What made Nancy so different from other white people I had met was her way of relating to a person of color as a person, first. In turn, I put aside my own worn racial clichés. It wasn't that we didn't see our racial difference; we just didn't let it blind us to the rest. The next day, she told me how much she enjoyed our conversation. "I told my husband, 'Janet and I are getting to be such good friends, we have to have her over.' I've never had a conversation like that with someone I've known for just two weeks . . . There's something about you." I'd met a very unlikely kindred spirit.

A solid cloud mass filled Seattle's sky and didn't budge for months. Fall was without sun and winter without snow. The dire warnings about the city's dreary, drizzly weather turned out to be true and I settled in grimly underneath the gray tent. The job was much less stressful than Worthing & Schuster and I liked the company of my colleagues. I worked, played tennis poorly, and socialized with new friends. Three road tests later, I got my first driver's license, something just short of the Holy Grail for a subway-trained New Yorker. The tank-like pale blue 1976 Ford Granada I saw on sale for seven hundred dollars suited me perfectly with its 8-cylinder engine and imposing girth. I named it the Blue Lagoon.

Spring brought Mother and Kevin for a visit. I took them to dinner in a restaurant atop the Seattle needle. They noted with pleasure how nice everyone was and how white people didn't seem afraid of them, as they did in New York. At the end of the vacation, Mother returned to Brooklyn and Kevin moved in. He was worried about the destructive pull of the projects on him and felt the need to get out of that environment. I was happy to have him around and got him a job in the mailroom of my law firm. We had great fun hanging out in my office, acting "project" behind closed doors and "proper" as soon as someone knocked. He learned to drive my car and got his license, too. I was glad to share with him a group of people he would never meet back home, which was the least that could be said about my odd assortment of friends. There was a Korean American rapper, a black male ballet dancer, a Samoan secretary, and assorted lawyers. Kevin grew particularly close to Annie, whom he called his "other big sister." One of twelve children, she had helped raise five younger brothers and treated Kevin like the sixth. Seven months later he moved back to New York. The lure of home proved too strong for him, but at least he had seen a different way of living, a world beyond the projects.

The day he left, I hid in his room crying as he and Annie packed luggage into the trunk of the Blue Lagoon, but I understood his explanation. "It's nice, but I want to be home." I was also longing for a place that felt more like home: Paris. Seattle was indeed a nice, eminently livable place, but for a New Yorker from the edgy side of Brooklyn, it felt like a hip retirement community for yuppies. It had given me the distance I needed to discover what I wanted for my life, and the picture I came up with was not of a cozy house, shiny car, and grinning kid in a backyard. I constantly thought about Paris, the most diverse city I knew, with its wealth of Asians, Africans, Arabs, West Indians, and a good number of African Americans. Since my junior year there, I had returned a few times on vacation and was always sorry to leave. I often daydreamed at work about narrow, shop-filled sidewalks, elegant churches, and teenagers break-dancing on the wide terrace of Trocadéro. In comparison, America's most livable city looked frightfully bland. Nonetheless, I continued to practice law, tried in vain to transform myself from an indoors to an outdoors person, and made the best of what Seattle had to offer.

Then Larry Zimmerman called from New York. The civil suit was finally coming up for trial, four years after its 1985 filing and ten years after the rape. I would never be over the rape, but I had gotten through it. The power I derived from my survival meant everything, and I would rather die than lose that small victory to a lawyer's greed and a misogynist's pathology. A rapist once conquered me with brute force. It was my turn to vanquish him with the kind of strength that truly meant something. I flew back to New York.

The trial was unsettling but not devastating. Seated once again in the witness chair, hearing the perpetual defendant once again snort and rattle his chains, I was filled as much with pity as with disgust. Paulette had volunteered to accompany me to take on "that fucking prick bastard" and returned his menacing stares with her own hate-filled gaze. His lawyer's absurd questions bored me. The raised voice, the accusatory gestures, the aggressive body language—all a joke. I was a lawyer myself by then and understood the game. It wasn't personal, because I wasn't a person. I was what stood between him and a third of twenty million dollars. The same cruel questions and sarcastic tone that hurt so much the first time around now seemed like the poorly rehearsed antics of a bad actor. The judge must have thought so, too; they lost.

I gradually resumed my Seattle life, all the while missing the style, culture, and beauty of Paris. The French were renowned worldwide for their cultural chauvinism, but skin color appeared to be of little importance to them. Among African Americans, they were known for their affinity for *our* culture, especially jazz and gospel music. There was the well-known Holy Black Parisian Trinity—Baker, Wright, and Baldwin. But there were many others who had lived there—the writer Chester Himes, the painter Faith Ringold, jazz woman Alberta Hunter, and Angela Davis. So why not me?

It had been a year since my last mailing of résumés to Paris. The lack of response was disappointing, and I stowed away that fantasy in the place of dreams—deep in my heart. I accepted my destiny not to live in France; I could always vacation from time to time, like so many other Francophile Americans. And that is precisely what I was doing in Paris the day I phoned one of the French lawyers who'd ignored my résumé. I wanted at least to make him feel guilty for not answering my letter. His first words stunned me. "Allo! Do you still want to work in Paris?" Of course I did! So much that I had stopped letting myself feel it. "Good. Then you come to my office tomorrow morning at nine for an interview." I was in Paris as a tourist, not a job seeker, and had neither résumé nor interview clothes. I hurriedly borrowed a skirt and blouse from a French friend, still in disbelief.

The next morning, I climbed the steps at the Arc de Triomphe métro station, a stop I told myself was an omen. The offices were a couple of blocks away, in a lovely century-old building. The lawyer was in a hurry and wasted no time on small talk. A position had opened up . . . The office needed someone immediately . . . French language skills . . . American law training . . . Before I had time to exhale, I was back outside, looking at the massive arch. As omens go, I couldn't have asked for better. I stood there and savored the moment. Mother had survived her fortieth year in the projects, Ann was celebrating a very hard-won sobriety, everyone was alive and out of jail, and I was moving to Paris. You could have knocked me down and fanned me with a brick.

EPILOGUE

We all seek a sense of belonging, a feeling of connection to something, yet each of us wants also to be special. Not an easy feat. This I learned early, for to be special in a large family, to stand out and sparkle, I cultivated the very trait that would later torment me—differentness. The more unique and different I became, the more isolated and lonely I felt. The conflict deepened when I ventured from the safely marked paths of family, class, and race into the tangled complexities of the educational system.

Who would dispute the error of requiring a child to leave her family, in the broadest sense of the term, in order to receive the kind of education that opens opportunities rather than shuts doors? Why were there trade schools but no academic high school in my own neighborhood? I don't mean to suggest that I regret the opportunities I was given—I am deeply grateful for them. But there are no free lunches. What I gained in possibilities was nearly out-weighed by my loss of grounding. The message I received as a child equated home with failure; fortune could only be found elsewhere, with people unlike me. The contrast between my actual back-ground and the worlds where I was sent to find role models was brutal. In such a situation, the natural reaction is to shift one's identification to those *others*. But, unlike many in that situation, I refused to let go of home. I wanted to stay true to people like me, true to myself. That is a sound choice. As we graduates of the underclass move through the doors opened by education, too many of us opt to let go of who we were, and of those who remind us of who we were when we began the journey. My mistake, however, was in my refusal to let my project-girl self evolve. I confused evolution with substitution and was constantly fighting off some phantom "white girl" I feared would slip in during the night and substitute herself for me. I nearly perished in the battle. Part of the problem was the ambivalence I felt around me toward both the value and the personal impact of schooling.

My parents' belief in education didn't change the fact that I was in a community that, for reasons tied to economics and its unique history, placed less value on academics than on other means of survival. I feared changing in ways that would make me no longer fit in in my world, a world that all too often equates academics with becoming corny, bookish. It amazes and saddens me when I go home that even now many people still think that way and subject school kids to the same ridicule I endured. This must change, or those who already have the least opportunity in society will be left even further behind.

It's been said that trauma is a "proving"—something that seeks and, if the heart and mind can bear it, will find the truth of a person, her essence. The greatest honor in suffering is to be able to redeem oneself through change and perhaps change others. My brush with violence compelled me to plumb my inner depths in ways I wouldn't wish on an enemy, but the exploration revealed to me my own capacity for such change. It also showed me the glaring flaws in our legal system at a time when I was a student of that system. Having grown up seeing friends go in and out of precincts, courtrooms, and prisons, I had thought of working as a criminal defense attorney after law school. That was before the rape. Watching a rapist go in and out of precincts, courtrooms, and prisons, only to rape again after each release, convinced me that I wanted nothing to do with a criminal justice system that makes such injustice possible. As a lawyer, I believe in the presumption of innocence and the right of an accused to legal representation and a fair trial. After all, I *am* a project girl, with friends who are convicted murderers and contrite muggers, spontaneous purse snatchers and scheming pickpockets. But mostly I know victims. And I believe in *our* innocence and our right to fairness, too.

My choice to live abroad may be a way of opting out of the struggle to belong: I have *chosen* to be a stranger. Here, I am free to focus my efforts on living who I am, not fitting into someone else's notion of who I should be. But I know where my heart is, and I *can* go home again, whenever I like. Mother likes to say, "You can take the girl out the projects, but you can't take the projects out the girl." That may not apply to everyone, but in my case it's true. And I would have it no other way.

ACKNOWLEDGMENTS

For helping to bring this book into being, I thank my Vassar sister Mia Goldman for the spark, Carol Mann for that first vote of confidence, and my editor Jonathan Galassi for his smooth and astute editorial touch. No expression of gratitude would be complete without shout-outs to my stateside homegirls Paulette Constantino, Annie Gleason, Charlotte Sheedy, Brandyn Barbara Artis, and Leah Jarrett for their realness, and to my fellow Parisians Laure de Gramont, Françoise Greisch, Léonide Honoré, Colette Modiano, and Lynn Bell for so much wisdom and inspiration. I thank Larry Zimmerman for his faith and mettle. And I am especially grateful to Gwen Wock for her humor, heart, and insight.